CONFESSIONS

OF A CATHOLIC STREET EVANGELIST

CONFESSIONS

OF A CATHOLIC STREET EVANGELIST

Frederick W. Marks

ISBN 978-1-940777-70-2

Joseph Reidhead & Company Publishers
www.reidheadpublishers.com
Augusta, Missouri and Yosemite, California

This book is set in Adobe Garamond. Designed by Robert Slimbach and released in
1989, Adobe Garamond is based on the roman types of Claude Garamond (c. 1490-
1561) and the italic types of Robert Granjon (1513-1589).

Cover photo courtesy of Patrick Sweeney

To Sylvia

CONTENTS

APPENDICES

ACKNOWLEDGMENTS

Like most books, this one could not have been written without the assistance and encouragement of kindred spirits.

There were times when I would have been hopelessly at sea had it not been for the help of my wife, Sylvia. She has given of herself in every possible way. My thanks, as well, to those who read the *Confessions* in manuscript form and offered valuable suggestions, among them Sr. Maria Veritas Marks, O.P. (my daughter); Fr. Donald Raila, O.S.B.; Piroska Haywood; Anne Carroll; Professor Ronda Chervin; and the Most Reverend John Oliver Barres, bishop of Allentown, Pa.

Four members of the Catholic Evidence Guild — Joe Traver, Don Murray, Gregg Kelly, and Pat Sweeney — pushed me to hone my apologetics skills on the floor of Grand Central Terminal, as well as at the crosswalks of some of New York's principal park sites.

Steve Dawson, the founder of St. Paul Street Evangelization, not only encouraged me to make frequent trips to the highways and byways; he furnished sandwich board signs, along with rosaries and tracts — all at reasonable cost.

Last, but not least, I wish to thank my editor and publisher, Joseph Reidhead, who has been the soul of patience, good counsel, and reliability.

INTRODUCTION

For every convert who joins the Catholic church in the United States there are four who leave. And among those who remain, few see themselves as evangelists. Jehovah's Witnesses, Mormons, and Evangelical Protestants continue to make dramatic gains in membership while Catholics have lost 3 million since 2007 in spite of heavy immigration from Catholic countries. According to the latest statistics, Catholics are the least interested of all Christian groups in Bible study. They also show the least interest in evangelization. A whopping 99.9% of the missionaries one is likely to meet on the street are non-Catholic.

Lack of interest in what St. Paul called "the sword of the spirit" is hard to fathom. One of the first things Our Lord did following the Resurrection was to lead a Bible study – on the road to Emmaus. He did it again after appearing to the apostles in the Upper Room.[1] We know, too, from the Acts of the Apostles how Christianity came to Africa. Deacon Philip led a Bible study for Queen Candace's treasurer on the road to Gaza.[2] The greatest Scripture scholar of all time, St. Jerome, was Catholic, and the biblical canon on which we rely was established by Catholic bishops at Catholic councils.

How can the faithful remain cool to Bible study when all the popes of the past hundred years have made a case for it, even going so far as to offer special indulgences? John Paul II urged Catholics to bring the Word of God with them on vacation, and Pope Francis, recognizing the importance of what he called "serious, ongoing study of the Bible," not only prescribed it for every parish, but recommended it to commuters on their way to work.[3]

Disinterest in evangelization is equally hard to fathom. All the leading nations of Christendom received their faith from missionaries commissioned by the See of Rome, and again there has been no lack of papal encouragement. Some fifty years ago, Pope Paul VI wrote that the Church "exists to evangelize."[4] The *Catechism* is even more emphatic, calling witness to the faith "necessary for salvation."[5]

John Paul II recommended a special kind of evangelization when he addressed a World Youth Day audience in Denver on August 15, 1993:

> Do not be afraid to go out on the streets and into
> public places, like the first apostles who preached
> Christ and the good news of salvation in the squares
> of the cities, towns, and villages. This is no time to be
> ashamed of the Gospel. It is a time to preach it from
> the rooftops.

Benedict XVI followed suit, as did Pope Francis, who began his pontificate by urging Catholics to take to the streets even if it left them "bruised, hurting, and dirty."[6] "How beautiful it is," Francis remarked, for young people to be "street preachers ... joyfully bringing Jesus to every street, every town square, and every corner of the earth."[7]

The papal appeal could not have been more timely. But, it fell on ears that were mostly deaf. As a member of the Catholic Evidence Guild, I can attest to the fact that when Catholics come to our table in Central Park or Grand Central Terminal and we offer them free literature to enhance their understanding of the Faith and equip them to pass it on to others, many act insulted. "I'm Catholic," they say – almost indignantly. And as often as not, they want to know: "Who authorized you? Does the Cardinal know about this? Since when do we have to advertise?"

During the 1990s, in order to make ordinary co-religionists the missionaries they are intended by their Creator to be, Mother Angelica launched her Eternal Word Television Network (EWTN), which has been a beacon to millions around the world. At about the same time, Fr. Benedict Groeschel revived the Catholic Evidence Guild after decades of inactivity, and Curtis Martin established the Fellowship of Catholic University Students (FOCUS) to lead Bible studies on campuses across the nation. More recently, Steve Dawson founded St. Paul Street Evangelization to empower men and women like you and me to take their faith to the public square.

The need, however, is for more Angelicas and Groeschels, more Martins and Dawsons. Above all, we need everyday Catholics who are anxious and willing to roll up their sleeves. Which is why this book was written. The first few chapters spell out the many ways in which every man, woman, and child, whether trained or untrained, can involve themselves evangelically. The rest of the text focuses on the nuts and bolts of street witness, laying out in detail what it takes to reach a wide range of separated brethren, along with members of other religions or the non-religious.

Why is such information needed? Because most churchgoing Catholics have been left in the dark when it comes to techniques of faith-sharing. One would never know, judging from the message coming from the average pulpit on Sunday, that pope after pope has asked for evangelization or that the Catechism *requires* it. The man in the pew knows that God wants him to be kind and caring. What he needs is a wakeup call informing him of his evangelical duty and explaining in easy-to-understand, down-to-earth terms how to bear witness to those whose spirituality has been bleached out of them by the mainline media. Stay tuned.

CHAPTER 1

EVANGELIZATION IS FOR EVERYONE

The word "evangelization" tends to conjure up images of Bible-thumping, hell-fire-and-brimstone orators thundering on soapboxes. But one doesn't have to mount a podium at Times Square to send a signal. Nor does one need high-level academic credentials. All that is required is a humble, willing heart. If, as Catholics, we take the Faith seriously, if we love Christ and His Church with every fiber of our mind, heart, and soul this light of ours will shine. In Pope Paul VI's words, "the whole Church is missionary," and he is seconded by Pope Francis: "all the baptized are agents of evangelization … every Christian is a missionary."[1]

Evangelization, broadly defined, is simply the bringing of souls to God, and there are countless ways of doing it. An invalid lying flat on his back in a hospital room can lift souls by being appreciative. A blind man walking down a street, cane in hand, can smile. Cheerfulness in the face of danger, optimism in the wake of disaster, serenity in the midst of turmoil – all bear witness to the liberating power of a God who is all-good and all-loving.

Two stories come to mind in this connection. The first occurred in the year 1888 at a Catholic leper colony on the Hawaiian Islands where Fr. Damien and his saintly co-worker,

Sr. Marianne Cope (since canonized), worked with extraordinary gallantry amid ghastly conditions. So great was the tenderness and good cheer with which they treated the victims of the dread disease that Robert Louis Stevenson, the author of *Treasure Island* and *Dr. Jekyl and Mr. Hyde*, was moved to write an immortal tribute:

> To see the infinite pity of this place,
> The mangled limb, the devastated face,
> The innocent sufferers smiling at the rod,
> A fool were tempted to deny his God.
>
> He sees, and shrinks; but if he look again,
> Lo, beauty springing from the breast of pain!—
> He marks the sisters on the painful shores,
> And even a fool is silent and adores.

The other story takes a more personal turn. My mother was diagnosed with multiple sclerosis in 1940, and although she was given only a year to live, God had other ideas in mind. She brought me into the world that year, and four years later she bore my sister against the advice of her doctor. For forty years, she endured creeping paralysis and prolonged pain. By the time she breathed her last, she couldn't feed herself or even swallow solid food. Yet, to the very end, she was the most cheerful member of the family, secure in knowing that God would never send her more trouble than she could handle. The memory of her joy, kindness, and humor in the face of adversity is more precious than anything else she could have left us. My father, who suffered from a serious hearing disability, was also a role model, never complaining, never anything but loyal as a husband and father.

Even if my parents had never said a word about religion their example was enough, in itself, to help me get through adolescence. It also inspired my sister to persevere in her battle against the enslaving power of alcohol and drugs – a battle she eventually won. However, my parents *did* say a word – *many words* – about religion, and their words, especially those of my mother, based on a life-long study of the Catholic faith, were powerful. It is hard to say which was greater, the verbal witness or the living example.

Daily, we engage people in conversation, and each occasion is a God-given opportunity. A pleasant word here or a note of cheer there can melt the coldest heart. People in my neighborhood tend to be pessimists, especially about the weather. If I say "It's a lovely day," they are likely to respond, "Yes, but it's supposed to rain tomorrow." To which I reply, "True, but after the rain, the sun will be back!" When it's raining and my nay-saying friends complain about "what a lousy day it is," I shoot back, "Come on! Every day, rain or shine – they all come from the same workshop!" When December rolls around and folks begin wishing me "Happy Holidays!" I tell them, "It's Christmas for me! The season of light!"

I remember when one of my neighbors, in response to my statement that life is wonderful, replied: "As long as you have your health." "Absolutely," I agreed, "but doesn't health come second after faith? Haven't you known healthy individuals who were miserable? And invalids who beamed? So tell me something. What's the secret of happiness?" Try this sometime with a smile. Then get out of the way to let the words penetrate. It takes time, generally, for a grace-filled moment to work its magic.

Folks are quick to lament the carnage left in the wake of a natural disaster, and when they do, I sympathize and try to put the tragedy in evangelical perspective, inviting prayer for the victims, but also for the thousands of innocent children slaughtered every day in their mothers' wombs.

How we handle a given situation depends, of course, on its "feel." The smoother we are, the better. But nothing ventured, nothing gained. Fluency comes with trial and error. The main thing is to be on the lookout for evangelical openings and, when one of them comes our way, to count on the help of the Lord, who will turn well-intended weakness to strength.

America is dying of thirst – spiritual thirst – and if we don't provide living water, who will? If our friends are mourning the death of a relative, we can ask them if they believe in an afterlife and quote St. Paul:

> Eye has not seen, nor ear heard, nor has it entered into the heart of man what God has prepared for those who love him.[2]

If they tell us they belong to another church, we can ask if they've ever considered joining the Catholic Church, and if they seem receptive, we can see if they have any questions about the Faith. In my own case, if they put me on the spot with queries I can't handle, I simply take down their contact information and get back to them.

Some folks will tell you they used to be Catholic or were raised Catholic. "Come on back!" I tell them. They need to know that the Church, with all of its problems as an institution that is human, as well as divine, has the fullness of the truth; also that it's the road to happiness for those who take it seriously (for a model follow-up letter, see Appendix E).

Not long ago, I stopped at a diner for breakfast. A waitress came over to my table to pour me some coffee, and she said, "Good morning." I replied, "Good morning. How're you doing?" and I shall never forget her answer: "Still blessed." The joy and serenity on her face, along with the evangelical message, made me want to jump up and give her a great big hug. I didn't, but I couldn't get over how, in two, non-wounding words, she had managed to convey a wealth of meaning: "God exists. He's helped me tremendously, and I believe He could help you as well."

A while back, a woman standing next to me in a supermarket checkout line brought up the subject of contraception. She'd just borne her first child and wanted us to know that it would be her last. "One is done," she pronounced. But just at that moment, the woman behind her spoke up: "Honey, every child is a gift from God!" Once again, I felt like hugging a perfect stranger! Could she quote chapter and verse from the Bible? Probably not. But no doctor of divinity could have been more eloquent.

The "apostolate of the word" has a vocabulary all its own. If we believe Jesus when He tells us that not a single sparrow falls to the ground without God willing it, then words like "divine" and "providential" will take the place of "fortunate" and "lucky." Likewise, if we view sex as sacred and the body as something given only in marriage, then the phrase "having sex" makes no sense. Marriages that last are about giving, rather than having. Why use the language of the enemy? Why not call premarital sex by its proper name, fornication, and sex that is licit "marital relations"?

The high priests of materialism are doing all they can to drive religion underground. They will never be satisfied until every last sign of God's presence is eliminated. One way of pushing back is to season our conversation with exclamations such as "God bless" and "God willing." It will take more than two or three well-chosen words to restore the Almighty to His rightful place. But the use of Godly language is sure to sow seeds, and these seeds will germinate, given the proper soil. If one hears, "What a wonderful day it is!" one can respond with a hearty "Amen" or "Praise the Lord!" And on parting with friends, one can wish them a "blessed day." Arturo Toscanini, arguably the greatest orchestral conductor of the 20th century, was not afraid to say, "God bless you" in professional settings where piety was anything but the norm.[3]

A list of all the ways in which the untrained can make a difference would stretch a mile long. Those blessed with the gift of making friends can use it to clear a path to men's hearts. One doesn't need a master's degree in theology to send a contribution to EWTN or boycott companies that advertise indecently while notifying them of our action and explaining why. One can thank a priest for giving a good homily.

Different folks, different strokes. Some will hang a rosary on their rear-view mirror. Others will wear a cross. Those committed to the apostolate of the bumper sticker may invite tailgaters to meditate on the words "God is Pro-Life." Just the other day, I noticed a large sign on someone's lawn. It turned out to be an ad for roofs, doors, kitchens, and a half dozen other things. I was struck by the contractor's versatility, but what really floored me was the way the ad ended: "John 3:16 and Dt. 6:4."

If I recall correctly, Jesus said that unless we acknowledge Him before men, He will not acknowledge us before His Heavenly Father (Matt. 10:33). Will our Christmas cards bear the image of a fir tree or a scene from the life of the Holy

Family? When dining out, will we begin the meal with grace? Oftentimes, evangelization hinges on a simple gesture. When I was growing up, people used to make the sign of the Cross when passing a church to show respect for the presence of the Blessed Sacrament. G. K. Chesterton (1874-1936), one of England's best-loved authors and a convert to Catholicism, not only crossed himself whenever he entered his study; he put a cross below his signature, as well as at the top of every manuscript page.

Whatever happened to wearing one's "Sunday best"? Psalms 29 and 96 bid us "worship the Lord in holy attire," and it is one of the few ways we have of letting the world know what we think of the Lord's dinner party. Have you ever wondered why Moses was told by God to take off his sandals at the burning bush? Our Creator demands outward signs of respect, and since one of the principal purposes of the liturgy is to give glory to God, is there not something incongruous about giving God the opposite of glory? How can one dress formally for a funeral that pays homage to a human being, but not for Sunday Mass that honors a Man who gave His life for us? Invitations for weddings and receptions stipulate "black tie" or "business attire" to highlight the importance of the occasion. But what could be more important than what happened – and continues to happen – at the Last Supper?

There are people who change into a suit before going to art museums because they regard such places as "sacred." One gentleman who dressed formally for a trip to New York's Metropolitan Museum wrote that "with all this incredible history and gorgeous work, I want to present myself properly. I just feel it's an honor and a tribute to the work."[4] When the New England Patriots and New York Giants football teams flew into

Indianapolis for their 2012 Super Bowl warm-up, they wore coats and ties.[5] Perhaps we have something to learn from basketball coaches, sports announcers, and the athletes themselves.

Few things are more telling than one's behavior at Mass. Crossing one's legs during the Offertory or draping one's arms over the back of the pew sends a signal, as does the practice of treating the sanctuary as if were a chat room. There are plenty of places to talk, but only one where Christ is specially present. The one time Jesus resorted to violence was when He was outraged by the spectacle of people disturbing God's "house of prayer."[6] If you talk during a musical recital, there's a good chance you will be shushed by your neighbor. And what applies to a concert hall applies a hundred times over to the house of the Lord. When listening to the still, small voice of God, one is easily distracted.

Do we risk being misunderstood if we tell chatterers politely, and with a smile, that "it's hard to pray when people are talking"? Yes. But listen to the psalmist:

> For your sake [O Lord] I bear insult, and shame covers my face ... because zeal for your house consumes me ... I looked for sympathy, but there was none, for comforters, and found none.[7]

The chit-chat could continue. We could be embarrassed (it's happened to me more than once). It happened to Paul, who was willing, at all times, to be a "fool" for Christ.[8] Mother Angelica is another person who found that "unless you are willing to do the ridiculous, God will not do the miraculous."

Returning, though, to the theme of the present chapter – namely, that one doesn't have to be theologically astute to be evangelically active – anyone can recommend books and CDs that are pro-Catholic. Anyone can pass out tracts. Early in the 17th century, Protestants in the vicinity of Geneva, Switzerland refused to hear the great Francis de Sales preach. So Francis, by slipping tracts under peoples' doors, converted 40,000! One of my friends rides the New York subways, and one of the things he likes best is to sit on a tract entitled, "Why Jesus Christ is Important." When he leaves the train, the person who takes his seat will find it and can read it if he is so inclined. Handing out leaflets on the street can be frustrating because takers are few and far between. But since when is truth concerned with how many people it convinces?

GOING DOOR TO DOOR

Doorbell ringing requires more in the way of coaching than simply handing out tracts. But again, it can be done by just about anyone. Members of the Legion of Mary have been at it for nearly a hundred years with nothing but good results. Going two-by-two, in imitation of Christ's disciples, they bring greetings from the pastor and a simple question: "Is anyone in your household a baptized Catholic?" There are four possible answers.

1. All in the household are baptized Catholics and belong to the parish. If this is the case, they say they're glad to hear it and offer inexpensive rosary beads, holy cards, or medals, along with tracts that explain the faith.
2. All are baptized Catholics, but they no longer attend Mass. There are thirty million Americans who fit this description, and the answer is a straightforward question: "Would you care to say why?" The visitation team is prepared for a brief

discussion of theological questions based on knowledge of the Catechism. But usually, the reason for non-attendance is personal, and if so, the team listens respectfully, indicating that a meeting with the pastor can be arranged to discuss the grievance. Finally, before leaving, they ask whether the pastor can call.

3.   No one in the household is a baptized Catholic and all are church-going Protestants. In this situation, the team offers congratulations and asks, "Have you ever had an interest in Catholicism?" followed by, "Do you have any questions about it?" Folks may bring up Church scandal or ask about veneration of Mary, the Real Presence of Jesus in the Eucharist, or the celibate priesthood. In which case, a brief explanation is offered, along with a leaflet.

4.   Finally, if the household is Muslim, Mormon, Jewish, atheist, or Jehovah's Witness, the team leaves a packet of tracts.

The main problem with door-to-door evangelization is not finding anyone at home – calls are not generally made during mealtime or after dark. But even when there is no one at home, one can leave a church bulletin on the doorstep with a note of explanation, and in a surprising number of cases, children are brought in for baptism, cohabiting parents are properly married, and visits by extraordinary ministers of the Eucharist are arranged. RCIA attendance is sometimes recommended for non-Catholics, and when the parties in question are assured that there will be no pressure, they may give it a try.

One of the best examples of evangelical faith-sharing occurred several decades ago. Ronald Reagan, the fortieth president of the United States, told Soviet leader Mikhail Gorbachev about a Soviet soldier in World War II who lay in a shell hole at midnight awaiting an order to attack. The soldier had never been a believer because family, friends, and teachers had told him that God didn't exist. But looking up at the stars and touched by their beauty, he voiced a prayer asking the Lord to accept him if he died. As it turned out, the prayer wound up in the hands of the soldier's widow, who sent it to Reagan.

Gorbachev's reaction to the President's story was what one would expect from a Communist. He tried to change the subject – to space travel. But Reagan, not to be put off, remarked that although space was close to heaven, it wasn't as close as some of the other subjects they'd been discussing! Whereupon, he made the case for God's existence based on the argument from design, telling Gorbachev that he wanted to invite his skeptical son, Ron Reagan, who didn't believe in God, to a gourmet dinner and ask him if he believed the dinner had a cook.

Going back even farther to when Reagan was a boy, the world's fastest runner, Olympian gold medalist Eric Liddell, used his fame and speaking ability to boost attendance at religious revival meetings. More recently Michael Chang, youngest man to win the French Open Tennis Championship, acknowledged God's help in post-game press interviews. Mariano Rivera, baseball's greatest closing pitcher, did the same in his autobiography.

If we have a name like Reagan or Rivera, the value of our witness increases exponentially. But as the popular hymn "Balm in Gilead" has it, "If you cannot preach like Peter, if you cannot pray like Paul, you can tell the love of Jesus." We can all testify, not only to Jesus' love, but also to our own love for Catholicism. We don't have to be a star athlete or president to tell others about the joy and lightness we have felt after a good confession. There is no one who can't bear witness to the fact that the Sacrament of Reconciliation, which involves critical self-examination, can be helpful in marriage on the many occasions when one must say, "I'm sorry."

If the Church has been a comfort to us during illness or bereavement, if we've been fortified against sin by frequent reception of Holy Communion, or if we have taken advantage of the Church's "open door" policy, which offers a haven off the busy street for prayer and meditation, we can say so. Has our faith enabled us to take an objective look at Marian apparitions such as those that occurred at Guadalupe, Lourdes, and Fatima? Think about it. As Catholics, we don't have to dismiss some of the greatest miracles of all time as "popular religion" in the face of overwhelming evidence to the contrary. If we consider ourselves blessed that it is a cross, and not a weathervane, that surmounts our church steeples, and if we regard the Church's steady adherence to the moral code of the Apostles over a stretch of two thousand years as a miracle, why keep it under wraps?

Are we proud of the Holy Father's reputation? Protestant evangelist Billy Graham called John Paul II "the strong conscience of the whole Christian world."[9] At a time when the industrialized nations of the West threw their weight behind a radical UN program for the promotion of contraception, abortion, and sterilization, a lone voice spoke out, that of John Paul II. The Pope was subjected to withering criticism. But his courageous stand won support from Muslim nations, as well as many from Central and South America, and in the end, sanity prevailed.[10]

It's time to get out the trumpets! The hospital originated with Catholics, as did the university, common law, and democracy. Florence Nightingale, an English Protestant recognized for her pioneer work nursing the wounded, had nuns as teachers, and there was a time in her life when she aspired to become a Catholic. The American Church educates, feeds, houses, clothes and cares for more people than any other non-governmental institution. Historically, it has led the way in ministering to the blind, the elderly, and lepers. St. Vincent de Paul (d. 1660) is the father of modern-day organized charity, Mother Teresa of Calcutta the best-known social worker of the 20th century.

Perhaps, in light of Church teaching, you had more children than you wanted. Perhaps, too, one of the "extras" turned out to be your pride and joy. Isn't this good news? Has the Church's prohibition of remarriage after divorce helped you keep your marriage vows? Has your hand as a parent been strengthened by the ability to tell your children that God put you in charge?

On the rolls of the Church one will find the names of the world's greatest saints, along with those of the most eminent philosophers and theologians of all time – men of the caliber of Augustine and Aquinas. Why not let people know?

FRATERNAL CORRECTION

We have yet to mention what may well be the most difficult part of our evangelical duty. According to Jesus, we are "the salt of the earth," and salt is a disinfectant; if it loses its potency it is of no use except, in Christ's words, "to be trampled under foot and thrown away."[11] We may be standing at a water cooler or sitting around a coffee table when the conversation turns suggestive. Paul tells us that nothing obscene or scurrilous should even be *mentioned*.[12] Is silence an option for Christ's salt? Perhaps we change the subject, or, failing in this, excuse ourselves with a parting jest: "The party is getting rough!"

Mother Angelica tells of the many times she felt "like a porcupine at a balloon party." Let's face it. No one wants to appear "holier than thou." We know, too, that because God alone judges souls we must be as merciful toward others as He is toward us.[13] One of the most popular subjects for homilies is Jesus' insistence on the need we have to remove "the beam" from our own eye before we go after "the speck" in the eye of another. And rightly so. One mustn't rush in where angels fear to tread.[14] Nor is there any obligation to cast our "pearls before swine."[15] Those whose attachment to heinous, unrepented sin leads them to deny the existence of absolutes may well be beyond the pale.[16]

But this said, fraternal correction, under ordinary circumstances, is a Christian duty, one of the seven spiritual works of mercy. The Gospel tells us plainly that if our brother sins we are to rebuke him, and if he persists in sinning we are to shun him.[17] Jesus Himself was a "sign destined for contradiction," and we, as His followers, must be brave, acting on principle even if it means being "hated by all."[18]

When profanity fills the air, one can respond by asking the person with the unhinged tongue, "Do you know this God to whom you refer? Are you familiar with the Second Commandment?"

Once, I was having my hair cut at an out-of-town barbershop when the man with the scissors kept up a steady stream of "Jesus Christ!" and "For Christ's sake!" Consternation welled up within me – to the point where I said, with the warmest smile I could muster, "Do you know this Jesus who is so often on your lips? Do you think He likes having His name taken in vain?" My words didn't register. The barber kept right on swearing, and I kept countering with, "There you go again!" When he finished cutting, I told him to skip the shave. His razor would have come too close to my jugular vein!

Oftentimes, people who are complete strangers will confess their sins in the course of casual conversation. One minute, they're telling you about their new car or how to get a discount on Thanksgiving turkeys. Then, out of the blue, you're hearing about a "significant other." Silence on our part is sure to be taken as a form of absolution when what they need, more than anything, is a frank expression of concern. If the "feel" of the situation allows, you might cite statistics indicating that most cohabiters break up, leaving one or both parties scarred (for those who marry, the divorce rate is significantly higher than it is for the chaste). Catholic apologist Ralph Martin, who has dealt at length with such issues, suggests that we try to bring the conversation around to the four last things – death, judgment, heaven, and hell. People should know that we want what's best for them in the long run, what will make them happy.

When the subject of abortion comes up, we may be in a position to remind our friends that God is at work on every embryo from the moment of conception, forming it into a person with a special mission and an immortal soul. And if those to whom we are speaking view Scripture as divinely inspired, we can quote God's words to the prophet Jeremiah, "Before I [God] formed you in the womb, I knew you" (Jer. 1:5), followed by Isaiah 49:15, "Can a mother be without tenderness for the child of her womb?"

There may be a price to pay since truth is heavy. Pray outside an abortion clinic, and you could wind up listening to a chorus of angry women chanting, "Keep your rosaries off our ovaries!" Ask for quiet in church and your piety could be taken for arrogance: "Who does he think he is? So holy, so religious!"

So be it. The Old Testament prophet Jeremiah, confronted by "terror on every side," and hearing shouts of "Denounce!" was hurled into a deep cistern with mud up to his neck (Jer. 20:10). Few of us are called upon to be another Jeremiah. But there are occasions when all of us must leave our comfort zone.

The second chapter of the Book of Wisdom offers one of the best descriptions ever penned of how a friend of God is likely to appear in the eyes of the world:

> "Let us beset the just one because he is obnoxious to us; he sets himself against our doings, reproaches us for transgressions of the law, and charges us with violations of our training. He professes to have knowledge of God and styles himself a child of the Lord. To us he is the censure of our thoughts; merely to see him is a hardship to us because his life is not like other men's and different are his ways. He judges us debased; he holds aloof from our paths as from things impure ... with revilement and torture let us put him to the test that we may ... try his patience. Let us condemn him to a shameful death, for according to his own words God will take care of him." These were their thoughts, but they erred, for their wickedness blinded them.

Anyone who stands for truth of any kind, be it secular or religious, is going out on a limb, because error hates the light. Louis Pasteur, who conquered anthrax, cholera, and rabies, had to leave Paris because the French scientific establishment held him in disdain. Ignaz Semmelweiss fled Vienna because a recalcitrant Austrian medical profession couldn't stomach his insistence on the need to sterilize surgical instruments. Had they taken his advice, child-bearing women could have avoided the deadly contagion of puerperal fever.

But why dwell on the difficulties when there are so many positives? "The greatest kindness one can render to any man," wrote St. Thomas Aquinas, "consists in leading him to truth." Once upon a time, a maidservant of Monica, the mother of St. Augustine, told her that she drank too much and was, in fact, becoming a sot. This was all Monica needed to begin her ascent to sainthood. St. Bernard had a vain sister who came to visit him at his monastery, and his refusal to see her put her on the road to conversion.[20] According to Proverbs, "He who rebukes a man gets more thanks in the end than one with a flattering tongue."[21]

I'm sure we've all had some surprises along this line. I once told a cohabiting Catholic that fornication is a mortal sin in the eyes of the Church – equivalent, without confession, to ex-communication. To my astonishment, he thanked me and, wonder of wonders, proceeded to marry! On another occasion, I slipped a note under the door of a cohabiting Jewish neighbor, informing him of the probable outcome of fornication (based on the latest statistics), and also quoting pertinent passages from the Old Testament. It didn't take long for my doorbell to ring. "Who do you think you are?" he demanded. "I'm your neighbor," I answered. "When I see a man blindfolded and headed for a cliff, I don't sit back and yawn. I say something." It wasn't long before he, too, married ... and we parted friends!

Even when we fail (or think we've failed) at fraternal correction the effort is eminently worthwhile because, like any other form of evangelization, it will strengthen our own faith. Remember the good thief on the cross, the one who rebuked his fellow thief at Calvary? There is nothing to suggest that his words of chastisement, uttered in pain, registered on his fellow thief. But one thing is certain. He pleased his Maker enough to be guaranteed a place in paradise, something unique in the annals of Christianity!

Perhaps the example of a good thief using his precious breath to rebuke a fellow thief is more inspiring than the thought of a blind man smiling or the memory of a mother bearing up under multiple sclerosis. But it matters little whether we picture ourselves as a good thief, a blind man smiling, a cheerful paralytic, or none of the above. Everything that we have said thus far falls under the heading of bringing souls to God, and none of it requires formal religious study. In the next two chapters, we will develop our theme at greater depth, suggesting ways in which the evangelical imperative applies to parents and pastors.

CHAPTER 2

THE EVANGELICAL PARENT

From day one, every parent is an evangelist because no one stands in greater need of conversion than a newborn baby. Although tykes lack the overweening pride of grown-ups, they are far from docile. A concerted effort must therefore be made from the start to see that they grow up proud of the Faith and knowledgeable enough to defend it.

Even before your newborn arrives, there are decisions to be made. One way of showing that you take your faith seriously is to name the child after a saint. But this is only the beginning. How often will you take the little one to church? We profess to believe in the Eucharist as the body and blood, soul and divinity of Jesus, just as we acknowledge its power to invigorate us spiritually. But if we attend Mass only when we must – once a week and on holy days of obligation – and if we don't take our children with us to make occasional visits to pray before the Blessed Sacrament where Jesus is specially present, how can we expect them to believe in transubstantiation? How much stock do we place in Catholic teaching? The Church claims infallibility on faith and morals. But if we regard ecclesiastical dogma as a smorgasbord from which we pick and choose, how can we avoid appearing hypocritical?

Frequent confession is recommended by the Magisterium – every six weeks or so. And again, if we limit it to once a year, what's the message? Better to bring the young ones regularly to the Sacrament of Reconciliation, stand with them in line, enter the confessional ahead of them, and tell them how refreshed we feel when we emerge because this way, we are giving them the wherewithal to mature spiritually.

How many times have we heard prayers offered on Sunday for religious vocations? As evangelical parents we must take it upon ourselves to encourage our children to remain open to God's calling, and one way of doing this is to invite a man or woman of the cloth to share a meal with us. Marriage is not for everyone. I once heard a father boasting about the fact that his five-year-old Johnny already had a girlfriend. Talk about parental pressure!

St. Brigid of Ireland (c. 450-525) was blessed with every conceivable gift – brains, beauty, and breeding. Her parents expected her to marry, and being a dutiful child, she wished to please. Deep down, however, she longed to give herself entirely to the Church. So she prayed for help from above, and it was not long in coming. A disfiguring eye infection put her suitors off and softened her parents. In the end, she succeeded in laying every one of her talents at the feet of the Lord. And what talents they were! She founded a double monastery (for men and women) at Kildare, which was, for centuries, a powerhouse of spirituality and culture. Imagine how many more Brigids we would have today with less worldliness on the part of parents. Cardinal Newman's lament should be our own, "Holy Angels and the blessed Saints are always crying, 'Alas, alas, and woe, woe!' over the loss of vocations, and the disappointment of hopes and the scorn of God's love."

The most valuable gift any parent can give a child, next to an intact marriage, is the example of virtuous living. No one is perfect, but if we are not honest, hard-working, temperate, and chaste, nothing we tell our children is going to register. Only when we keep our promises, defer to our spouse, admit mistakes, and forgive injuries will they learn what God is like and what He expects of His sons and daughters.

Consider asking your young ones not only what they learned at school, but also how they behaved themselves. They need to know that worldly success is not the family god. Were they kind to an unpopular student? Did they thank their teacher for a stimulating class?

The hardest part of parenting is discipline. But from what I remember of my own upbringing, I would never have made it to manhood on a steady diet of hugs and kisses. Children need limits, along with encouragement, and part of this is letting them know that you will go the distance to enforce whatever rules you lay down. Just as God is mercy and justice alike, parents must be the same. Children are fortunate if they grow up in a home where there is zero tolerance for profanity, where lying is treated as the serious sin that it is, and where Jesus' equation of lustful looks with adultery is sincerely taken to heart. They need to know, early on, that the body is the temple of the Holy Spirit and that immodesty and the wrong use of makeup attract the wrong kind of attention.

The Church has always taught that parents are the primary educators of their children, especially when it comes to faith and morals. And this is because they will foster respect for human life by addressing hot-button issues with reserve and dignity. Because every child is different, the "one size fits all" instruction found in many academic settings, particularly those that are co-ed, can be harmful. Parents have a right to know what is going on at school so they may have their children excused from instruction or activities that are objectionable. In exercising their God-given prerogative, they may incur the wrath of the principal. Letters of recommendation for college entrance could be withheld. But blessed is the child who witnesses heroic sacrifice on behalf of a just cause. When Mom and Dad show that they are willing to run risks in accord with Jesus' promise "Seek first the kingdom of heaven, and all these things will be added to you" (Matt. 6:33), it will do their brood a world of good.

If regular schooling turns out to be an abomination, some thought might be given to homeschooling. It requires time and energy, along with a certain degree of competence, and much depends on state regulations, which vary. In certain regions, there are no requirements at all. The trend is toward deregulation, and the number of homeschooled children, over two million at present, is on the rise with results that are generally excellent. Those who learn at home under parental supervision rank 15 to 30 percentile points above public-school students on standardized tests, and they are three times more likely to have strong Christian beliefs.[1]

One of the greatest advantages of homeschooling is its avoidance of public sex education. But regardless of where your child goes to school, there is no reason why you can't instill respect for the sanctity of human life. Patronage can be withdrawn from smut-peddling magazine shops or filling stations and the owners told why you are boycotting them – with your children at your side. Let the proprietors know that porn is more dangerous than a loaded pistol because it threatens the life of the soul, which is immortal. If a film turns out to be indecent, you can walk out with your youngsters in tow – or better still, go to the box office in advance and find out what you are letting yourselves in for (for a list of classic films that are both decent and entertaining, see Appendix G).

There is no reason why screen actors and actresses should have to disrobe before the camera. Why is it that fig leaves were not enough to satisfy the Lord? Why did He give Adam and Eve special clothing and tell the Israelites, "You must not be indecently uncovered"?[2] In the Old Testament, Shem is praised for covering his father's nakedness, and in the New, nudity is associated with demonic possession.[3]

Modesty is one of the twelve fruits of the Holy Spirit – so vital that the Catechism devotes four separate sections to it (beginning with #1832). Jesus, speaking to this very point, said we must become like little children if we are to enter the kingdom of heaven. "For adults only" is the way nudity is described by the mainline media. Striptease joints are "gentlemen's clubs," sodomy is "gay," and film producers are entitled to "artistic license." Surely, there is no better proof of the accuracy of Scripture wherein Satan is described as the "father of lies" disguised as an "angel of light."[4]

Teach your children four basic principles of love and marriage, and they will be set for life: (1) sex, which is about babies, is sacred because human life, made in the image and likeness of God, is sacred; (2) if human life is sacred, then the institution that protects it (marriage) is sacred as well; (3) contraception not only adulterates the marriage act, it leads to an even greater evil, abortion, which is murder; (4) those who contract a valid union may never, under any circumstance, divorce and remarry – not for illness, not for alcoholism, not for physical abuse, not even for infidelity. The Church allows separation in extreme cases, but never remarriage during the life of the spouses except in cases of annulment, in which case a "marriage" was never valid to begin with.

You will want to steer your children toward peers who share their values, and if there are no kindred spirits at school, you must look elsewhere. If you discriminate, friends and relatives may tell you to "lighten up." It may affect your child's popularity. Worry not. Few things are more dangerous than an unchecked craving for human respect. How are children to know that worldly goods and worldly power are not first on your list of priorities? In Arthur Miller's play *Death of a Salesman* Willy Loman, the protagonist, asks his sons if they are "well-liked" at school – as if this were the be-all and end-all – and before the curtain falls, Willy, who is at once a liar and an adulterer, commits suicide.

One reason we tend to be uncomfortable with "discrimination" is that some of those whom we are duty-bound to shun may be close relatives. Jesus had the same problem. His kinsfolk, thinking Him mad, tried to reason with Him, and His response, quintessentially Christian, was intended for us: "Whoever does the will of my Father in heaven is my brother and sister and mother."[5] Yes, Christ dined with sinners. But the so-called "sinners" – Zacchaeus, the tax collector, and Mary Magdalene – were repentant. Furthermore, Jesus did not regard the dinners in question as social affairs, but rather as occasions when the Doctor of Doctors would heal men and women humble enough to admit a need. That the Divine Physician came in His professional capacity is clear from the way He lectured His hosts, "You gave me no water for my feet … You gave me no kiss … You did not anoint my head with oil."[6] One of those who received Him was taken to task for not inviting a broader cross-section of society, and He improved upon the occasion by suggesting that Jews could not count on automatic admission to God's dinner party.[7]

Nowadays, few are familiar with this other side of Christ – a side that finds an echo in the outlook of early churchmen. John the Evangelist, hearing that a heretic had entered his bathhouse, urged his companions to leave "lest even the bathhouse fall down because Cerinthis, the enemy of truth, is within."[8] This was the same John who rebuked the church of Pergamum for its failure to expel defenders of fornication, who condemned the church of Thyatira for not excommunicating a loose woman, and who praised the church at Ephesus for its hatred of sexual immorality.[9]

It was simply the way things were during apostolic times. When St. Polycarp, Bishop of Smyrna, ran into the heretic Marcion on the streets of Rome, he minced no words. Marcion asked, "Do you know who I am?" and Polycarp replied, "the first-born of Satan!"[10] St. Ignatius, Bishop of Antioch (d. 107), another example of evangelical intolerance, forbade any association with Christians whose ideas on grace and the Eucharist were heretical.[11] If we read the Acts of the Apostles, we find that when Simon Magus asked Peter if he could purchase his miraculous powers, the Fisherman told him, in no uncertain terms, that he and his money could go to hell.[12] Five chapters later, we find Paul calling Bar Jesus a "son of the devil" and striking him blind for raising objections to Christian teaching.[13]

One can go further. Paul devotes an entire chapter in one of his letters to the need for Christian discrimination, making clear that those who were notoriously wicked were to be excommunicated.[14] Paul's list of the kind of people who qualify for the term "wicked" is interesting; it includes gluttons, drunkards, the incestuous, the quick-tempered, adulterers, thieves, the violent, the insolent, the brutish, the grudging, lovers of self, lovers of money, the idle, the ungrateful, the disputatious, slanderers, and dissenters from Church teaching, to name but a few.[15]

Given the attitude of Christ and His apostles, one is not surprised to find the Didaché (circa 60-100 A.D.), the earliest of Christian conduct books, advising its readers to "keep away from every bad man." In like vein, The Shepherd of Hermas, another apostolic favorite, maintains that "the greatest amount of honey is ruined by the smallest amount of wormwood."

This, dear reader, is not a book about shunning! But it is important to know that from the very start, the Church of Christ was divinely intolerant, as well as divinely inclusive. The early Church opened its doors to Gentiles and social outcasts. Tax collectors, Samaritans, and reformed prostitutes were welcome. We know that Paul treated the slave, Onesimus, as if he were a son. On the other hand, this was not a church that gave comfort to the wicked or one that expected good to overcome evil through association. Sirach, the conduct book of the early Church, holds that "he who touches pitch shall be defiled, and he who associates with an impious man learns his ways."[16]

Did things change over time? Yes, but the change was slow in coming. Sixteen hundred years after Christ, Francis de Sales was urging his followers to avoid the company of immodest persons. Add another century, and St. Jean Baptiste de la Salle, founder of the Christian Brothers, was warning that "nothing can be more dangerous than evil companions" since "they communicate the evil of their vices to all who associate with them." As late as the third quarter of the 19th century, St. John Bosco could compare bad company to a "dangerous disease" and tell the boys under his tutelage that "a rotten apple will rot every apple in the basket."

Today, the situation is altogether different. When cohabiters go off on a cruise and relatives are asked to water their flowers or walk their dog, the answer is apt to be yes. When a Catholic gets divorced and remarries outside the Church, relatives are likely to attend the wedding. They should stay home. It is this very issue that Jesus addressed when He reminded His followers that loyalty to God comes before family ties: "Do not think that I have come to send peace upon the earth; I have come to bring a sword, not peace ... to set a man at variance with his father, and a daughter with her mother ... He who loves son or daughter more than me is not worthy of me."[17] Statistics indicate that a more widespread refusal to sanction illicit marriage would be a boon to society because close to 70% of all women who are divorced, and 60% of men in the same situation, regret their decision within two years of breakup.

When a grown child shacks up without benefit of marriage, many parents will lower their standards rather than run the risk of estrangement. The tail ends up wagging the dog. What a fallen child needs to hear from parents may be simply stated, "We will respect you as a person and keep you in our prayers. But we can't invite you for dinner unless you come alone because the breaking of bread signifies a unity that is sorely lacking. We cannot, in good conscience, support behavior that is heinously wrong." A breakdown in communication between the generations is sad, but sadder still is complicity in sin. The father in Luke's parable of the prodigal son is kindly and forgiving, but a doormat he is not. There is no killing of the fatted calf until the son begs pardon.

False tolerance is the besetting and besotting sin of our age. During the late 1940s and 1950s, atheistic Communists lobbied for a "marketplace of ideas," and the idea seemed good at the time because it was thought that Americans of every party and opinion should have an opportunity to express themselves. There were to be no more witch-hunts. Over the years, more and more forms of censorship were discarded. But the desired outcome has eluded us. Instead of a marketplace of ideas, what do we have? The pendulum has swung in the opposite direction – to the point where disapproval of almost anything except intolerance is forbidden and witch-hunts are on again, only with a new class of "witches": pro-life pharmacists, nurses, doctors, and politicians.

Getting back to the makeup of an evangelical home, if you find that your children have two thousand friends on Facebook, you have a right to object. Their time is better spent doing other things. Laptops can be screened against porn. TV can be reserved for special programs.

One of the best ways of instilling virtue in children is by teaching them to appreciate beauty because truth, goodness, and beauty are interrelated. Foster one and you foster all three. Introduce youngsters to great film, along with classical music and the art of the masters, and they will sense the abiding presence of God, who is the source of all creativity. Certain children's books are attractively illustrated, as well as instructive, and this is another plus since it is a come-on to visual, as well as literary, beauty. Many a convert will tell you that their first attraction to Catholicism was the splendor of a Gothic cathedral.

Nature has a beauty that far transcends anything found in museums. It is also free, with lessons to teach. The natural cycle of life, death, and rebirth, as experienced in seasonal climes, prefigures our own life, death, and resurrection. We can't always take children to places of scenic grandeur – mountain lookouts, lakes, and the seashore. But we can teach them the names of trees and flowers. They can pick up acorns, chestnuts, and smooth white pebbles – all free, once again, for the taking. If you exult in the magnificence of sunset and sunrise, if, in a word, you show them the work of the world's greatest Artist – the symmetry, the balance, and the divine harmony – it will foster a faith in absolutes, and as they grow older they will be more likely to turn their back on ugliness.

Ideally, the evangelical home will be neat and cheerful, with holy images to remind family members of the Christian ideal. Faith-building CDs and DVDs, along with works of apologetics, spiritual reference books, and lives of the saints will grace its shelves. For bedtime reading, there will be Bible stories. Catherine Vos' *Child's Story Bible* is outstanding for its coverage of the Old Testament (see Appendix F for other suggestions), and five minutes a day of New Testament reading will furnish the family with impressive evidence for the truth of Catholicism.

There's an old saying, "The family that prays together stays together," and it coincides with John Paul II's estimate of prayer and fasting as "the first and most effective weapons against the forces of evil."[18] For prayer, there will be a special place in the home equipped with a candle and a set of rosaries where conversation with the Lord is held at regular intervals. For mortification, there will be abstinence from meat on Friday in remembrance of Christ's passion unless some other form of sacrifice is substituted, as mandated by the Church. Foregoing dessert one day a week or even an entire meal as a mark of solidarity with the Our Lord's passion and death will yield savings that can go to charity.

If your child asks why we fast, you can begin by explaining that fasting is a token of our belief in the lordship of the soul over the body, even as it tests the power of reason over passion. It expresses sorrow for our sins, as well as for the sins of those who may be converted through our sacrifice. It is also commanded by Our Lord who went forty days in the desert without food.[19] John the Baptist fasted, as did Paul. In the Old Testament, Moses and Elijah mortified themselves for forty days as precursors of the Lord.

LOOKING OUTWARD

We haven't yet gotten to the missionary function of the evangelical home, but not because spiritual outreach is unimportant. Evangelical Catholicism without public witness of one kind or another is simply a contradiction in terms. One possibility is volunteer work on behalf of the poor and underprivileged. Another is street evangelization of the kind popular with non-Catholics. Why should our Protestant brethren have a monopoly on verbal outreach when we have the fullness of the truth? A third option is anti-abortion demonstration. The annual March for Life in Washington, D.C. which attracts hundreds of thousands from all over the country, packs a political punch. Congressmen and senators have windows on the Mall!

Whatever you decide to do, be real. If you say that abortion is murder but do nothing about it, what are your children to think? Or if you tell them evangelization is vital without lifting a finger to spread the Good News? Youngsters have an eye for phoniness.

LOVING THE LORD WITH ALL ONE'S MIND

Even if your children attend a Catholic school, a certain amount of homeschooling can be helpful with an eye to teaching them how to love God with all their mind, as well as all their heart and soul – something required by Jesus. Part of what's required could be the memorization of key Scriptural passages such as Matt. 16:18-19 and John 3:16; 20:22-23, along with the Nicene Creed, the Ten Commandments, the Seven Capital Sins, the Corporal and Spiritual Works of Mercy, Mary's Magnificat, and the opening verses of the Gospel of John. If the youngsters are first-rate scholars, you might offer them a prize for mastery of the Sermon on the Mount (Matt., chapters 5-7).

At public schools the mere mention of God's name can be held against a student. But even at a Catholic institution, children may be misinformed about certain things such as the inerrancy of Scripture. Complaining to the teacher is unlikely to accomplish anything, and administrators, even those who are sympathetic, may have their hands tied. In my own case, I felt I had to ask my daughter at the end of each school day what she had learned in religion class, and if it ran counter to the truth, as it sometimes did, I would get out the Catechism or an encyclopedia of Bible difficulties and provide a corrective. I also told her she could preface her answers to exam questions with the disclaimer, "According to what I heard in class ..." No student should have to spout heresy in return for a passing grade.

THE FIVE-POINT BRIEF FOR BELIEF

Peter bids us to "be ready always with an answer to everyone who asks a reason" for what we believe.[20] Loosely paraphrased, this means that all of us, along with our children, must be familiar with apologetics. But again, this is not something youngsters are likely to get on their own, even at a Catholic school. There are a number of good apologetics texts, and one can spend considerable time going through them. But the case for Catholicism boils down to a five-point brief for belief:

1. Jesus claimed to be God (for proof texts, see Appendix A under "divinity");

2. He proved it by the miracles He worked, culminating in His Resurrection from the dead (John 5:18,23; 8:58; 20:28);

3. He established a Church (Matt. 16:18-19);

4. Catholicism conforms to all the New Testament specifications laid down for the Church of Christ (spelled out in ch. 5);

5. Scripture, upon which the first four points are based, is reliable – the evidence for the inerrancy of the Gospels is overwhelming (more on this in subsequent chapters).

The word "apologetics" may be off-putting because it sounds like "apologies," but there is nothing apologetic about the use of Scripture, Church history, and the Catechism to defend Catholic belief. Some fear that religious study of any kind, but especially Bible study, will raise questions that are unanswerable. Fear not! Scripture exhorts us to grow in knowledge so that we will be less prone to be "carried away by the error of the foolish."[21] The more one learns about Catholicism the more one loves it. And the more one loves it, the more one wants to share it. The deeper one delves into Scripture, along with the writings of the Church Fathers, the more one appreciates the *Catechism*.

Missing pieces of a divine jigsaw puzzle turn up around every corner. This one fits. That one fits. They all fit!

If your children are intellectually gifted and strong in the Faith, they may benefit from attending an elite out-of-state institution. More and more parents, though, are electing to keep their children home after secondary school – not only to save money, but also to keep better watch over their offspring morally. Freshman dorm life on many of today's campuses can be downright ugly. Recently, I heard of a case involving several girls who were chosen by the dean of their college to room together. One of them insisted on having her boyfriend with her overnight, and there was nothing to be done about it. School authorities, after refusing to intervene, wouldn't even allow like-minded students to apply for room reassignment during the second semester.

Finally, a word to the wise. If children are given the impression that they are not wanted at home, if parents tell them, "When you're eighteen you're out of here," they will look elsewhere for attention, and they may find it in places where you don't want them to go. So long as they are respectful and willing to contribute to the welfare of the family, they shouldn't, as a rule, be pushed out of the nest.

CHAPTER 3

THE EVANGELICAL PASTOR

We cannot give back to our priests the smallest fraction of what we owe them. They feed us with the Eucharist. They absolve us from sin. "Were we to realize fully what a priest is on earth," wrote the Curé of Ars, "we would die – not of fright, but of love."[1] Some of the nation's best minds and hearts are commissioned officers in God's army, and the same is true of the sisters who consecrate their lives to the Lord as teachers, nurses, and prayer warriors. Many among the clergy are incredibly generous, and if serious persecution were ever to come our way, they would be the first to suffer.

But this said, not every priest is truly evangelical in the sense of being visibly virtuous and demonstrably in love with the Lord. As John Paul II observed, "the priestly vocation is essentially a call to holiness."[2] Not every pastor educates. He may be a great fund-raiser; he may organize activities for folks of various ages and ethnic backgrounds; he may attract a huge following. But if he fails to form his people spiritually, they will be ripe for the blandishments of the world, sitting ducks for non-Catholic evangelization. Quoting again from the writing of John Paul the Great, he must have "a loving knowledge of the word of God and a prayerful familiarity with it... . [Priests] should immerse themselves in the Scriptures by constant sacred reading and diligent study," [and] "the first and fundamental manner of responding to the word [of God] is prayer." "The priest must also be a 'teacher of prayer,'" John Paul goes on, but he will only be able to train others "if he himself has been trained in it and continues to receive its formation."[3]

Sustained prayer, in short, is the wellspring of holiness; and holiness is what is needed to educate and inspire. Which is why Bishop Fulton J. Sheen, the greatest convert-maker of the 1950s, recommended an hour a day before the Blessed Sacrament. According to Sheen, the Holy Hour not only sanctifies, imparting the courage necessary to preach the unvarnished truth; it also generates ideas for sermons. Sheen knew whereof he spoke!

The pastor who is holy will not embroider prescribed Mass texts or dispense with the washing of hands – cafeteria Catholicism on the altar breeds cafeteria Catholicism in the pews. His altar servers and sacristans will bow or genuflect before the tabernacle. His ushers will be well attired, and he will see to it that there is a tranquil setting for Eucharistic adoration.

One of the age-old customs of the Church is the wearing of the Roman collar. Mandatory for official functions, it cheers believers, and, for non-believers, it invites questions that can lead to conversion. George Weigel calls it "a powerful sign to the culture of the imperial autonomous Self that there are things worth dying for – including things worth dying-to-self for."[4] There is nothing intrinsically "wrong" with sisters and priests traveling incognito. I myself have benefited from the love and expertise of many who have made this choice for reasons that are understandable. It is just that the wearing of clerics can be tremendously helpful. One of the first acts of an atheistic regime is the outlawing of religious garb because the wearing of clerics, from a totalitarian standpoint, sends a dangerous message: "God exists and the greatest joy this side of heaven is found in His service." Parishioners will take their cue from the pastor. If he is willing to "show the colors," they will be less likely to fly under the radar in the workaday world. Like the good padré, they will be proud of who they are and willing to pay the price of discipleship.

One might add that the wearing of Roman collars by priests and habits by nuns is no more traditional than a great many other things connected with the religious life. Formality militates against division, and if history has anything to say about it, Catholicism has been a formal affair from the start. Each of the seven sacraments has prescribed rubrics. There is a way to offer Mass and a way to design a church. Even outside the Church, there is a procedure for selecting a jury and conducting a trial. Congress goes by *Robert's Rules of Order*. In athletics, there is good form and bad form.

One of the more frequently asked questions these days is why the Eucharist should not be dispensed to non-Catholics. This is because the breaking of bread is a sign of unity that, in this case, is lacking. If, therefore, a nuptial Mass is being offered with guests in attendance who are ineligible to receive, the wedding program should contain a notice in bold type along the lines of the following:

> We are all reminded that to receive Holy Communion in the Catholic Church is to receive the **true body and blood** of Our Lord and Savior **Jesus Christ.** It is not a symbol. And owing to the holiness and unitive significance of the Sacrament, **only** those Catholics living in a state of grace (i.e., free from mortal sin) may receive. Catholics who have not made a proper confession and who are not prepared to receive the Blessed Sacrament as well as those from non-Catholic Christian churches

and communities should remain seated – they are welcome to use the prayer of spiritual communion found on the next page.

Prayer of Spiritual Communion

My Jesus, I believe that You are in the Blessed Sacrament. I love You above all things, and I long for You in my soul. Since I cannot now receive You sacramentally, come at least spiritually into my heart. As though You have already come, I embrace You and unite myself entirely to You; never permit me to be separated from You.

Since there are always guests who do not read, the instructions should also be read aloud from the pulpit.

If there is an anti-abortion prayer vigil in the neighborhood, the evangelical pastor will support it. If he hasn't time to join the march in person, he will encourage others. In his homily that day, he'll laud the participants, particularly the sidewalk counselors who are unsung heroes. Those who resign judgeships or county clerkships rather than issue licenses for same-sex unions will again be recognized. In the world of nursing, medicine, and pharmacy many have risked their livelihoods to avoid complicity in abortion. All of them should have a place on the Catholic honor roll.

THE KEY TO FAITH FORMATION

One day, a gentleman came up to me on the street and told me that the Church had let him down. When I asked him why, he said that Marian devotion in the parish where he grew up had taken the place of Bible study, apologetics, and training in evangelization. I replied that Mary herself would be the first to sympathize since she was a scholar, according to tradition. Then I continued as follows:

> If anyone would want quality RCIA, Bible study, apologetics, and training aimed at equipping parishioners to be a Catholic presence, both on and off the street, it would be the Blessed Mother. And I suspect that she would also want to see a copy of the *Catechism*, along with a Bible, in every home even if they had to be there at the expense of the pastor. I can also hear her saying, "Parishioners should be encouraged to devote at least five minutes a day to spiritual reading, beginning with the Gospels, the acts of the Apostles, Paul's Firsts Letter to the Corinthians, and the Letter of James."

This said, I threw the ball back into my interlocutor's court:

> Don't you think faith formation is partly the responsibility of the parishioner? Must one be wealthy or a genius to obtain a copy of the Catechism? What does it take to seek the counsel of a holy priest? When we don't find what we need in one parish, are we not free to go elsewhere?

Finally, I let the ex-Catholic know that while I wouldn't choose a parish that focused exclusively on Marian devotion, neither would I enroll in one that slighted the Blessed Mother, given the Bible's clear teaching that she is our Mother and Queen (more on this later).

SUNDAY HOMILIES

There is only one thing more important than the points we have been discussing, and that is what happens, or fails to happen, during Sunday Mass. Pastors intent on strengthening the faith of their flock will use their once-a-week "quality time" to deliver homilies that are morally and intellectually nourishing. Jesus' Sermon on the Mount is too long to compress into a twenty-minute talk, but in terms of what it prescribes, it is a great model – fasting, evangelization, almsgiving, sexual purity, and marital fidelity are but a few of the many subjects covered, and there is no doubt about what is being taught. The fact that the most famous sermon ever preached contains no less than four references to hell suggests that many of the "feel good" homilies presently in vogue leave something to be desired.

There is an urgent need for catechesis. As Fr. McCloskey and Russell Shaw point out in *Good News, Bad News*, "the state of Catholic attitudes" is "profoundly disturbing." As of 1999, the percentages of those who thought one could be a "good Catholic" without obeying Church teaching on abortion or believing in the Real Presence of Jesus in the Eucharist were 53% and 38 % respectively.[5]

Since the pastor, like every other priest, bears the title "father," he should do more than encourage his children. He needs to ride herd on them, knowing that goodness is the only thing that will make them happy in the long run. If the congregation is spiritually immature to the point of being unable to take heat from the pulpit, the approach may have to be gradual. When Paul took charge of the Corinthians, many of whom were wildly heathen, he fed them "milk" at first, rather than "solid food," to gain a foothold in their affection.[6] But by the time he finished with his flock, he must have been doing the same thing that he did later in Ephesus where he preached the Faith "in its entirety" – i.e. not skirting issues of sexual morality.[7] Felix, the Roman procurator who had Paul under lock and key, was astonished to hear his prisoner speak to him not only of justice and judgment, but also of chastity.[8]

There are various ways of feeding one's flock with milk, rather than solid food, as a starter. One of the pastors whom I know weaves hot-button issues into his Prayers of the Faithful. His people pray:

> that **civil society will recognize marriage** as a unique institution with the proper ends of unitive love and procreation; that the **contraceptive mentality, which has destroyed so much of family life,** will be replaced by a desire to bring children into the world so that married couples may, once again, enjoy the beauty of family life; that there will be an **increase in priestly and religious vocations** and that those who accept these vocations will do so with faithfulness and dedication; **that all human life will be respected** and protected from the moment of conception until the time it is called home by God; **that all abortion bills** will be defeated and that efforts being made to curb this evil will be successful; that **embryonic stem cell research** and the evil coming from it will cease and that the funds being appropriated for it will dry up.

Additional prayers are offered for many other intentions, including the sick, the suffering, the terminally ill, the faithful departed, and the souls in purgatory who have no one to pray for them.

The pastor's column on Sunday, still another vehicle for faith formation, could contain something along the following lines (found in the bulletin of an upstate New York church):

> BE CAREFUL OF STORMS: The biggest danger with any storm is that it will cause us to take our eye off the road. We may see lightning or trees bent by the wind. Suddenly, we have to slam on the brakes to avoid a crash. In our personal life we can also be sidetracked by secondary issues: Will my daughter still like me if I tell her it is wrong to move in with her

boyfriend? If I, as a priest, explain why abortion or contraception is wrong in one of my homilies, will my parishioners leave? If I seek reconciliation with a friend who has wronged me, will I be sorry? The list goes on and on, but Jesus reminds us to keep focused on doing and saying the right things: "Seek first the kingdom of heaven, and all things will be added unto you" (Sermon on the Mount). God will be pleased to have you on His side, pleased to have you passing on His teaching without watering it down. Just remember that it is Jesus before whom we must all stand on judgment day. He will be the judge of our conduct, not our children, not our friends, not government leaders. Some day, others will bear witness to the example and teachings we gave them. May their testimony be positive. May they say that we were faithful to God's commands.

The approach is up to the pastor. But if people do not hear about vital issues of sexual morality on a regular basis, they will succumb to worldliness, and when election day rolls around, they will vote their pocketbook.

All too often, the sole criterion for the success of a pre-Cana conference or a parish mission is popularity. The pastor is happy as long as no one is "scared away." Christ scared a whole lot of people away when He told them they had to eat His body and drink His blood (John 6). Was He lacking in pastoral sensitivity? Since when is religion a numbers game? "My people perish for want of knowledge," thundered the prophet Hosea at a time when the Jewish religious establishment was sacrificing truth to popularity and "feeding" on the sins of the people. Ezekiel, another voice crying in the wilderness, likened the priests of his age to shepherds who were pasturing themselves, rather than their flock.

When the celebrant at Mass describes God as "nothing but love and mercy" without reference to justice and judgment, which are "the foundations of his throne" (Ps. 97:2), he is leading people astray. When he lists the qualities of the good man as compassion, generosity, and tolerance with nary a word about chastity, honesty, industry, or fraternal correction, he is complicit in sin. How can purity, truthfulness, and hard work be thought of as vital if they are never mentioned? There is little difference between the priest who does nothing but dilate on God's love and the father of a family who lectures his children on the need to be polite while failing to tell them not to play with matches or drink Clorox.

It is hard to quarrel with kindness and neighborliness, familiar themes in today's pulpit. But as stand-alone messages, they will not suffice. To be caring and compassionate without being virtuous in other ways will not stand. Those who cohabit or abort while running soup kitchens are on the fast track to hell. In the words of Pope Francis, "We have had enough of immorality … It is time to acknowledge that lighthearted superficiality has done us no good."[9]

The gospel of niceness, preached without reference to the seven capital sins, is extremely popular. The man in the pew regards himself as not only nice but also as a saint. He hasn't killed anyone. He hasn't stolen. He has been a good neighbor. He has donated to Catholic Charities for the relief of unfortunates. He may even chair welfare committees. In a word, he is decent. The problem is that Hitler and Stalin could make the same claim when their stars were on the rise. They, too, were "decent" – at least in the eyes of their people. National Socialism and Communism were designed to meet the needs of the poor.

Margaret Sanger of Planned Parenthood, one of the nation's leading eugenicists and racists, sought to help the downtrodden. Euthanasia pioneer Jack Kevorkian claimed that his methods would enable people to "die with dignity." There is a world of difference, however, between the work of Margaret Sanger and that of Mother Teresa of Calcutta, between the suicidal mission of Jack Kevorkian and that of Jeanne Jugan, who founded the Little Sisters of the Poor. The difference comes down to a code of morality that affirms the sacredness of every human life regardless of race, class, creed, or color – from conception to natural death.

In short, there is no substitute for homiletic faith formation. An annual series on the Ten Commandments, followed by another on the seven capital sins, and still another on the spiritual, as well as the corporal, works of mercy would do a world of good. One homily out of fifty-two explaining the difference between venial and mortal sin and stressing the benefit of frequent confession would be golden. There should also be room during the year to focus on the four last things: death, judgment, heaven, and hell.

It goes without saying that good preaching, like alcohol on an open wound, is going to sting. A priest can tell whether or not he is doing a good job by the number of complaints he receives! Some of his people may switch parishes to sit at the feet of a preacher who sets them at ease. On the other hand, there may be potential dropouts who remain in the parish on account of the spiritual sustenance they and their children are receiving. Some may even raise their level of support. And there may be outsiders who add their names to the parish registry because they are hungry for the truth.

The standard excuse for milk-and-water sermons is based on the premise that "what folks don't know won't hurt them." As if there was no such thing as conscience and the natural law! Jesus hit this nail on the head in one of His parables. Remember the master who goes on a journey and leaves his servants in charge of his household? Some are briefed on the behavior expected of them in the master's absence while others aren't. When he returns, he finds all of them misbehaving, and what is interesting is that he has *all* of them scourged (Lk. 12:48). Although the uninstructed receive fewer lashes than those in the know, they are still punished because they should have known better on the basis of common sense and the natural law.

Make no mistake about it. The pastor who lulls his parishioners into spiritual slothfulness will have to answer for it. As Paul puts it, he will be guilty of their "blood" (Acts 20:26). He will also be responsible for any temporal consequences that may ensue. Abortion, for example, wreaks havoc on a woman's mental health and can be lethal, while cohabitation undermines the ideal of permanent commitment, which is the foundation for a happy marriage.

Timing is important. Those who wouldn't normally darken the door of a church are likely to put in an appearance at Christmas and Easter – CEO Catholics (Christmas and Easter only) – and what they need to hear, above all else, is that absence from weekly Mass without sufficient cause endangers the soul. Most are unaware that the weekly Mass obligation is Scripture based and required under pain of mortal sin by a Church with Christ-given authority to bind and loose.[10] As persons suffering from spiritual malnutrition due to their habitual absence from the Holy Sacrifice, they should get to confession and return to church so they can give glory to God, feed on the Word of God, along with the Eucharist, recite the Creed, and pray for the repose of deceased relatives and friends – things that are done at every Mass. I remember one homilist who put it in the form of a question: "Suppose you went for weeks on end without taking a shower or eating a meal? The hygienic and dietary needs of the soul are much like those of the body, only more pressing."

As an aside, is it not a mystery why daily Mass is hardly ever recommended? Many of the marquis signs standing outside churches list Sunday Masses only. And why shouldn't daily Mass be offered at a time when the average working man or woman can attend? One would never know that Catholics are strongly encouraged by the magisterium to receive the Eucharist daily.[11]

GOSPEL PASSAGES THAT CALL FOR COMMENT

Just as there are certain days like Christmas and Easter that call for special homiletic treatment, so, too, in the case of Scripture readings. Take, for example, Matthew 16:18-19. Peter, and Peter alone, received the "keys" to the Kingdom, and the commission given by Christ to His lead apostle is the basis for Catholic belief in papal teaching authority! Or take John 20:22-23. The Sacrament of Reconciliation was Jesus' first order of business following the Resurrection, and He "breathed" this life-giving power on the apostles. The only other time God breathes on man is when He breathes life into Adam through his nostrils! The message? Mortal sin brings death to the soul, while the Sacrament of Reconciliation restores it to life. Our Church is one of the few Christian organizations that acts on Jesus' commission – one more instance of Catholic conformity to biblical specifications – and again, the man in the pew needs to know.

EVANGELIZATION

We come finally to what Paul VI referred to as the pastor's "primary responsibility" – the spreading of the Good News. Will there be a sign outside his church inviting inquiry: "Have You Ever Considered Becoming a Catholic?" Will there be pamphlet racks at the rear of the church stocked with informational material for non-Catholics who wish to learn more about the Faith, as well as for Catholics who are spiritually illiterate.

Among the titles that have gone like hotcakes in my own parish and which can be downloaded from the Catholic Evidence Guild web site are the following: "Why Catholicism for All Christians?"; "Salvation Possible Outside the Catholic Church?"; "Are the New Testament Gospels Reliable?"; "Faith That Jesus Christ is Truly God is Reasonable"; "Jesus Christ Truly Rose From the Dead"; "The Host at Mass: Jesus Truly Present or Symbolic Memorial?"; "Why Scripture Alone? Why Faith Alone? Why Good Works Alone?"

If the pastor has an evangelization committee, his job will be that much easier. Committee members can xerox tracts, fold them, and refresh the display racks at the rear of the church. If, in addition, they commit to Bible study and apologetics courses, they can be a presence on the street and go door to door if the pastor is so inclined. From time to time a display table could be set up outside the church offering free information on the Faith. Finally, if there are questions that committee members are unable to answer, an "Inquiry Night" could be run by someone trained in apologetics.

Homilies making the case for evangelization are urgently needed because American Catholics tend to regard evangelization as a Protestant thing. Many are under the impression that example is all one needs to spread the Faith. If I had a dollar for all the times St. Francis of Assisi has been quoted as having told his followers, "If necessary, use words," I'd be a millionaire. Ask Franciscan scholars about this, and they will tell you that their founder never spoke or wrote as quoted. Even if he did, it would have been merely to state the obvious: that what one *does* is as important as what one *says*. To be sure, example is important. But, as St. Paul pointed out, "faith comes from what is heard."[12] Francis trained his men to be street preachers, even as he risked his life crossing enemy lines during wartime to convert the Egyptian sultan.

How much would the early Church have accomplished if its members had relied on example alone? Peter and his fellow apostles took to the street in obedience to Christ's command to "go into the whole world and proclaim the good news" (Mark 16:15). They were scourged. One of them, Stephen, was stoned to death for saying things that were politically incorrect.

Another myth making the rounds is the idea that charitable work is a substitute for verbal witness. Like an aircraft, Catholicism has two wings, social service and evangelization, and both are needed if the Faith is to fly. No one can deny that Jesus ministered to the needy. Without doubt, this is a Christian imperative. But it is not the only one, nor is it necessarily the most important. The primary mission of Our Lord while He walked the earth was to *teach*.[13] This is what He expected of His followers, and when He said, "The harvest is great, the laborers few," He was referring to a shortage of evangelists, not social workers.[14]

Had he opened a soup kitchen on the road to Emmaus, it would be one thing. Instead, He led a Bible study to prepare His apostles for evangelization. And when asked about love of neighbor, He put it second on His list of priorities after loving God "with all one's heart, mind, and soul."[15] After receiving the Holy Spirit at Pentecost, Peter told his listeners that he and his associates had been charged to "testify," and this is what they did.[16] If the first Christians had concentrated on the needs of the poor and simply set a good example (*solum exemplum*), the Church would not have grown as rapidly as it did.

In John Paul II's play *Our God's Brother* one of the characters, Adam Chmielowski, is driven by the force of conscience to do all he can for the poor, and his example is a noble one. Wojtyla's work is first-rate drama. But for every play about the world's Chmielowskis, we should have one touting the courage of those who followed in the footsteps of Dominic, Francis Xavier, and Mother Angelica. We know, too, that when Wojtyla became pope, he did a great deal to advance the cause of verbal witness, urging Catholics to take to the streets.

THE EVANGELICAL BISHOP

We have yet to touch upon the responsibility of a Catholic bishop. But, like the priest on the local level, if he falls short when it comes to the spiritual formation of his flock, he will have to answer for it. He may run hospitals and orphanages. He may pull his diocese out of the red, put an end to church scandal, and lower the boom on pro-choice politicians. But if this is all he does, it will not have been enough. In John Paul II's words, the bishop is the "pre-eminent catechist of his people," one who "must demonstrate his concern through direct interventions aimed at promoting and preserving an authentic passion for catechesis."[17] Unless he provides orthodox Bible study for his flock, along with training in evangelization, and sees to it that the Catholic institutions under his aegis are truly Catholic, his victories will have been hollow. And it is not only a matter of exhorting others to sound doctrine; he must refute those who contradict it.[18]

Diocesan institutions that are not what they ought to be need to be shaken up and revamped. It is not enough for a Catholic school to stress kindness and community service. It may offer weekday Mass, confession, and release its students for religious holidays. But if the faculty doesn't defend the reliability of Scripture and present Church teaching on sexual morality with clarity and candor, its graduates will be hard put to stay the course spiritually, much less win souls for Christ. If its hallways ring with profanity, if its chapel is used as a classroom or for storage, if lectors and extraordinary ministers of the Eucharist at school Masses are not chosen for their virtue and knowledge of the Faith – if, in other words, there is a disconnect between what the school professes to believe and how it operates – students will view the Church as insincere, and it is an impression they are likely to carry with them for the rest of their lives. At the same time, if there are Muslim or atheist students in the classroom who might be inclined to embrace the fullness of the truth, it will make their choice more difficult.

All too often, parents choose Catholic education for the wrong reason. It might be a good idea if, before enrolling their children, they were given a form to fill out signifying their willingness to have their offspring exposed to Church teaching on the seriousness of the weekly Mass obligation, along with the sinfulness of cohabitation, contraception, abortion, divorce, and sodomy. Alec Guinness, the British comic actor who had the world in stitches during the 1950s and 1960s, grew up Protestant. But when he sent his son to an elite Jesuit school, the principal warned that the boy might become a Catholic. Guinness ran the risk, and the result is history. The son converted, and so did the father.

The American bishops have a curriculum for high school students, along with a textbook series that fulfills the requirements of that curriculum. The problem is that parochial schools in financial need are apt to adopt public school texts subsidized by the state, and such books are likely to be subversive where the humanities are concerned. There is a need, therefore, for corrective supplements. Students would be well served by the appointment of a diocesan education committee charged with grading school texts for fidelity to the Faith – those, in particular, that deal with history, English, biology, and sex ed. Committee members must be knowledgeable in apologetics and tough-minded because, if they aren't, youngsters will wind up with views that are inimical to the Faith. Hot-button subjects such as the Crusades, the Spanish Inquisition, and the trial of Galileo call for careful, balanced handling that takes account of the context of the times.

Graduates of Catholic schools should know enough about the Roman Empire to be proud of their Church for championing the rights of women, eradicating slavery in western Europe, and ameliorating the lot of unfortunates. They should be aware of the fact that all the leading nations of the world were evangelized by missionaries commissioned by the Holy Father and know that the greatness of these nations is traceable to their Catholic roots. They should know, in addition, that Dante, Michelangelo, Christopher Columbus, and Wolfgang Amadeus Mozart, among others, were not only the greatest of the great in their respective fields; they were devout Catholics. Louis Pasteur,

France's premier scientist, prayed the rosary. Shakespeare, too, was a Catholic if one credits the latest research.

Needless to say, the bishop must look beyond his secondary schools to the seminary to ensure that apologetics, Scripture study, and homiletics are accorded pride of place. Pre-Cana preparation falls under his supervision as well. Unless cohabiters preparing for marriage are told why the Church regards fornication as a mortal sin and are instructed to separate for a minimum of six months they will be short-changed. Unless they are given good reasons for regarding sex as sacred, the Church's claim to infallibility on matters of procreation will ring false. Some will continue to call themselves Catholic, but they will be so in name only, and the moment they think it socially or economically advantageous to leave the Church, they will do so.

Homiletics is another area that lies within the purview of the bishop. If there is total silence on controversial issues, he may need to issue some guidelines as there are fifty-two weeks in a year and no shortage of Mass texts to draw from. If nothing else, the man in the pew would benefit from what Pope Francis has said about the gay/lesbian agenda and the systematic killing of infants in the womb: "Abortion is the death penalty for the unborn," and "Agitation for same-sex marriage is a war against God, a maneuver of the devil."

Last, but not least, the bishop would do well to see that his pastors are involved in evangelical outreach, and not only to lukewarm Catholics, but also to members of other faiths or no faith at all. Vatican II's *Lumen Gentium* talks specifically about a bishop's responsibility to care for non-Catholics and non-Christians in his diocese. In 1951, San Diego bishop Charles Buddy spearheaded a diocesan-wide doorbell ringing campaign. Ninety-five thousand non-Catholic homes were visited, and

Buddy's teams were welcomed ninety-five percent of the time. Six thousand persons expressed interest in learning more about the Faith; 5,000 converted; and nearly 10,000 lapsed Catholics returned to the fold.[19] Not all pastors had the time to involve themselves personally, and so they opted for lay leadership along the lines of the Legion of Mary model (as outlined in Chapter 1), and untrained missionaries invited questioners to an information forum at the church hall.

No man, even if he is a bishop, can eliminate every form of malfeasance. Clerical reform has never been anything but an uphill battle. But, as John Paul II remarked, bishops should be encouraged by the lives of the saints who were themselves pastors.[20] Charles Borromeo, 16th century Cardinal of Milan, risked his life for the cause of diocesan reform. One day, a disgruntled priest walked up to him, musket in hand, and fired at point-blank range. Miraculously, the bullet failed to penetrate, leaving only a bruise. Charles carried on as if nothing had happened, telling his priests, "our duty and office is to look out for [spiritual] dangers as from a watchtower and to repel them when they threaten those who are resting under our charge ... if any are being corrupted ... to heal them with the sharpness of salt; if any be wandering in moral darkness, we ought to hold the light before them."

In today's terms, "holding the light before them" calls for a refusal to give Communion to pro-choice politicians. According to Canon Law #915, people who have turned their back on Church teaching must be turned away from the table of the Lord, barring public recantation. There was a time when the Church distanced itself from crime syndicate leaders, even those who were Catholic in name, burying them, if at all, on a low-key, private basis. Abortion is no less serious as a sin than racketeering, and far more heinous than racism. Yet imagine the outcry if a notorious anti-Semite were allowed to receive Communion.

What to do? Pray that the U.S. Conference of Catholic bishops will agree on the need for greater discipline, also that the Holy Spirit will descend on seminary teachers, pre-Cana instructors, and pastors. We need a whole new mindset in many quarters about what it means to be Catholic.

CHAPTER 4

BARRIERS TO EVANGELIZATION

Human nature, fallen as it is, ensures that evangelization will always be difficult. "Quarry the granite rock with razors," wrote Cardinal Newman, "or moor the vessel with a thread of silk, then you may hope with such keen and delicate instruments as human knowledge and human reason to contend against those giants, the passion and pride of man." Given today's conditions, the challenge described by Newman is especially great. The Christian West has tasted the fruit of worldly success for longer than most of us can remember, and good times engender pride and debauchery.

Diane Moczar, an authority on Western civilization, describes the present generation as "the most difficult in history to evangelize" because "sexual immorality is rampant on a scale that would have scandalized a pagan Roman. Secularist assumptions inform all our public institutions. Ubiquitous media distractions have robbed this generation of the ability to think clearly, follow arguments, and concentrate for long periods. There is no historical parallel that I can see for such formidable obstacles to belief coming together at the same time."[1]

A DEARTH OF FAITH

Only a person acquainted with history can appreciate, to the fullest extent, how far we have fallen as a faith community. Few figures at the time of Christ were as self-serving as King Herod, but even he seems to have had enough faith in the supernatural to believe that a man whom he decapitated could rise from the dead.[2] Such a notion would be totally foreign to the mind of a modern politician. Today's villagers would not mistake missionaries for gods, as did the people of Lystra when they were visited by Paul and Barnabas.[3] During the apostolic age, few Jews questioned the possibility of demonic possession, and those who witnessed miracles were moved to glorify God.[4]

Turn the clock back seven hundred years, instead of two thousand, and one finds the same difference. Shops in medieval England were closed from December 25 to January 6 in observance of a two-week religious holiday, and one was duty-bound to receive the Eucharist eight times a year (on all of the principal feasts). Attorneys expected God to vindicate the innocent by enabling them to walk barefoot over red-hot ploughshares if they opted for trial by ordeal. In short, miracles were expected. No longer. We may not have reached the point of spiritual demoralization to which Christ referred when He asked: "When the Son of Man comes [to judge mankind], will He find … faith on the earth?"[5] But we seem to be well on our way, judging from the prevalence of a host of debilitating myths.

MYTH #1:
SITUATION ETHICS

In 2005, before his election as pope, Cardinal Ratzinger told a papal conclave in Rome that "we are moving toward a dictatorship of relativism which does not recognize anything as for certain, and which has, as its highest goal, one's own ego and one's own desires." Another name for the aberration is situation ethics, the notion that moral standards change with changing times and circumstances. As a misguided Hamlet says, "There's nothing good or bad but thinking makes it so" (Act 2, Scene 2).

Going by the rules of logic, relativism is self-contradictory because its claim that there are no absolutes is itself an absolute. It also runs counter to Scripture. In the Old Testament, the Book of Malachi states, "I the Lord do not change"; Isaiah assures us that "the word of our God stands forever"; and the testimony of the psalmist is equally clear, "All your commands are permanent [O Lord] ... you have established them forever."[6]

In the New Testament, Jesus teaches that "Scripture cannot be set aside"; also that "not one jot or tittle from the law [i.e. the Ten Commandments] will pass away until all is accomplished. ... My words [i.e. teachings] will not pass away."[7] Paul, echoing the Master, holds that "Jesus Christ is the same yesterday, today, and forever" and "all Scripture is inspired by God and useful for teaching, for reproving, for correcting, for instructing in justice."[8]

Yes, there are rules in both testaments that no longer apply – abstinence from pork, for example, and Paul's insistence on head coverings for women in church. But these are non-essentials having little to do with the Ten Commandments or the moral law of the prophets. The question is how to distinguish

Scriptural prescriptions that are essential (i.e. timeless) from those that aren't. And the answer is found in the sixteenth chapter of Matthew: Christ established a Church to act as a guide in these matters, and Peter (i.e. the pope), under the guidance of the Holy Spirit, speaks for the Church.[9]

For those who are unmoved by logic, impervious to the dictates of common sense, and unimpressed with Scripture, there is always history. Human nature has never changed, and there are moral principles that have been universally accepted – e.g., "thou shalt not murder," "thou shalt not steal," "thou shalt not commit adultery," and "thou shalt not bear false witness." During the 1920s, the anthropologist Margaret Mead published a book on Samoa in which she depicted the natives as totally uninhibited sexually and, at the same time, guilt-free. Her point: morals, being a function of culture, will vary, depending on time and place. Mead's book became a bestseller read by generations of college students, and she was invited to teach at Columbia University. Only later was it learned that she knew little about the language of Samoans and next to nothing about their way of life. While on the island, she stayed with an expatriate American family, and the natives she interviewed gave her the answers she seemed to want. In point of fact, the morality of the Samoan people was remarkably similar to that of Americans of the 1920s – strongly in favor of virginity before marriage and chastity thereafter.

MYTH #2:
RELIGIOUS INDIFFERENTISM

Around the time that Americans were embracing Mead as a sociological guru, the nation entered its first phase of religious indifferentism. A slender volume entitled *Mere Christianity* by Oxford don C. S. Lewis made a strong case for Christianity. It was a tour de force of apologetics, and it makes great reading even today. But it lulled millions, including many Catholics, into making light of sectarian differences. Suddenly, it was fashionable to be more interested in other peoples' religion than in one's own. Words like "heresy" and "apostasy" vanished from the popular lexicon. G. K. Chesterton (1874-1936), next to Newman the best-known English convert to Catholicism, called false ecumenism "the virtue of the man without character." "We haven't lost our pride as humans," he observed, "but we are proud of the wrong things such as modesty in matters of religion ... Modesty has moved from the organ of ambition [and] ... settled upon the organ of conviction, where it was never meant to be. A man was meant to be doubtful about himself but undoubting about the truth; this has been exactly reversed."[10]

Long after Chesterton, John Paul II condemned religious indifferentism in his encyclical *Redemptoris Missio* (1990). The demon, however, is still alive. When Lewis published *Mere Christianity* (1943), Christians had much more in common with one another than they do today. Protestants and Catholics may have differed on divorce and artificial contraception. But if you told someone in those days that the Christian world was headed for division on such issues as abortion, same-sex "marriage," and the ordination of women, they would have thought you unhinged. We see now that anything short of the truth in all its fullness is fraught with danger.

One of the byproducts of false ecumenism is a tendency to discourage would-be converts. Scott Hahn, who came to Catholicism from the Presbyterian ministry back in the 1980s, tells about the time before his conversion when he was advised by a priest to stay where he was!

Indifferentism can also foster a knee-jerk acceptance of apostasy. Oftentimes, when children leave the Church, parents fall silent in the interest of family harmony. Their progeny may seem happier, even holier, as non-Catholics than they did growing up, and, as the argument goes, "If it works, why buck it?" There is an element of truth in this. If our offspring, after an earnest search for the truth, are driven by conscience to embrace another religion, that may be exactly where they belong, at least for the time being. We know that all who seek the truth with a sincere heart will be saved. But this should not be the end of it. Like Monica, who refused to let Augustine, her erring son, go in peace, we should pray for the return of our loved ones knowing that Jesus wants everyone, without exception, to come to the truth (1 Tim. 2:4). Prudence may dictate what subjects we discuss over Thanksgiving dinner, but there are many ways of voicing concern. Tracts can be forwarded, for example, along with books and CDs.

Apostates may seem happy, but appearances can be deceptive. Again and again, we read about serial killers who were regarded as genial and well-adjusted before they went on the rampage. But let's say, for the sake of argument, that apostates *are* happy. They could be even happier, as well as healthier and more productive, as reverts. To argue otherwise is to embrace relativism, which again has no basis in Scripture.

Early Christian leaders were as one when it came to the urgency of belief in Jesus and the Church He founded. Nowhere in the New Testament is there the slightest justification for the "I'm OK, you're OK" brand of thinking. Old-line Judaism was a path to heaven for those who took it seriously — we know that all of the Old Testament patriarchs and prophets are in heaven (Luke 13:28). But with the coming of Christ came a call for change. Jesus presented the religious leaders of His time with a stark choice: either they changed their views or they were on the road to damnation.[11]

Paul's message to those who refused his invitation to convert could not have been more emphatic, "Your blood be upon your heads!"[12] Luke states in the Acts of the Apostles that those who were on the road to salvation were also on the road to Christian affiliation – a telling assumption.[13] As for Peter, he told his listeners, including many who may have been happy as Jews, that if they wanted to save themselves from a perverse generation, they must be baptized (Acts 2:37-40). Later, standing before the high court of the Jews with his life on the line, the first pope warned an irate audience that there is no salvation *through anyone but Jesus.*[14]

There is an answer for indifferentists who point to the existence of an estimated 30,000 Christian denominations, all claiming the guidance of the Holy Spirit and all differing in what they teach. Tell them to imagine two scenarios:

1. They are back in school. An essay question on one of the exams elicits fifty different answers from fifty different students, and the teacher grading the exam finds that all of the answers save one are poor to mediocre. The one that gets an "A" is the Catholic answer!

2. They are at a racetrack. Well-informed spectators place bets on different horses. But in the end, only one horse wins – the Catholic horse!

Disagreement among the many, even many who are wise and well-informed, does not preclude the existence of absolute truth.

The consistency of Catholic teaching on faith and morals for two thousand years, along with its resistance to the forces of division that were anathema to Paul, is nothing short of miraculous.

MYTH #3:
RELIGION IS A PRIVATE MATTER

The airing of religious views at social events has always raised eyebrows. But the current notion that faith is a private matter goes a step further. It is a spin-off from the idea that there is no such thing as moral absolutes. Sex, which should be private, is everywhere on display, while religion, which is nothing if not societal by nature, is kept under wraps.

How preposterous! Remove the missionary element from Christianity, and it is gutless. Just as there can be no salvation for those who don't seek it, neither can there be salvation for those who don't seek to share it. We spread the Good News because this is what Our Lord commanded, but also because faith is a perishable commodity – like happiness, it will not keep unless it is shared. As Scott Hahn has written, "When we evangelize others, we evangelize ourselves."[15]

MYTH #4:
ONE MUSTN'T ARGUE

Closely related to the myth that religion is a private matter is the notion that one shouldn't argue – "live and let live," as the saying goes. In his best-selling book, *How to Win Friends and Influence People*, Dale Carnegie held that the best way to win an argument is not to have one – "win an argument, lose a friend," he maintained. Carnegie had a point. But when something as vital as religion comes up in casual conversation, people should not only be permitted to speak their minds, it should be expected – provided that they do it in a friendly, non-confrontational way. Candor need not lead to acrimony! An intellectual tug of war can be invigorating. We may have to listen to some blather and settle for not making all of our points, but folks need to know that we are willing to go the distance. Avoidance of confrontation eliminates the element of risk. But it can also convey the impression that we are on shaky ground intellectually and that there's no such thing as objective truth, only "your truth and mine."

Jesus was fairly direct when He told the Samaritan woman at the well that her people had lost their way religiously.[16] He let the Sadducees know that they were "entirely wrong," and by the time He went to the Cross, He had argued all of His adversaries into silence.[17] Granted, we're not Jesus. But we are supposed to walk as He walked (1 John 2:6). Peter converted 3,000 by means of argumentation; Stephen "disputed" with naysayers; and Paul, who harangued every Jew willing to listen and debated in every synagogue willing to grant him admittance, told a hostile audience that they were "unworthy of eternal life."[18]

Every day, Protestants who are well versed in the Bible make converts by means of argumentation. Jehovah's Witnesses and Mormons do the same. Why should we, as Catholics, hold our tongue?

MYTH #5:
ONE MUSTN'T "IMPOSE" ONE'S IDEAS

Evangelization imposes nothing on anyone. It merely offers ideas – much the way Ford Motor Company offers cars. In the marketplace of ideas, the customer is free to choose. Ask your skeptical friends what happens when Congress passes a bill or when lobbyists use their influence. What happens when a president issues an executive order? There would be no political parties if folks foreswore democratic methods of persuasion. Voting is nothing if not an attempt to realize one's vision of a just society; the struggle for political and commercial dominance is an integral part of American life, and truth-bearers should not opt out.

Pope Paul VI, in his 1975 apostolic exhortation, *Evangelii Nuntiandi*, put it succinctly:

> Is it then a crime against others' freedom to proclaim with joy a Good News which one has come to know through the Lord's mercy? And why should only falsehood and error, debasement and pornography have the right to be put before people and often unfortunately imposed on them by the destructive propaganda of the mass media, by the tolerance of legislation, the timidity of the good and the impudence of the wicked? The respectful presentation of Christ and His kingdom is more than the evangelizer's right; it is his duty. .... It would be useful if every Christian and every evangelizer were to pray about the following thought: men can gain salvation also in other ways, by God's mercy, even though we do not preach the Gospel to them; but as for us, can we gain salvation if, through negligence or fear or shame – what St. Paul called 'blushing for the Gospel' – or as a result of false ideas, we fail to preach it? (#80).

The Church, as a church, has never approved of forced evangelization. When Charlemagne forced Saxon conversion at sword point, it was against the advice of his spiritual adviser. The Spanish Inquisition is often portrayed as an attempt to impose the Faith on non-Catholics. But Isabella's trials did not interfere with the Jews in their synagogues or the Muslims in their mosques. The only people tried were non-Catholics suspected of seeking to infiltrate Church and state by claiming to be Catholic.

The Protestant socialite Elizabeth Ann Seton, who broke with Episcopalianism in the early 1800s to enter the Church, was later canonized for her role as foundress of the parochial school system. What is interesting is that members of the Filicchi family who took her in and comforted her after she lost her husband to tuberculosis on a trip to Italy, leavened their hospitality with evangelical zeal. In addition to showing kindness, they provided her with Catholic reading material, including proofs for the Church's teaching authority written out in Filippo Filicchi's own hand. And when she asked Filippo, "If there is but one [true] faith and nobody pleases God without it, where are all the good people who die out of it?" Filippo replied, "That depends on what light of faith they had received. But I know where people go who can know the right faith if they pray for it and inquire for it and yet do neither."[19]

Bishop Cheverus of Boston is another example of a saintly person who didn't hesitate to lean on Elizabeth, advising her to join the Catholic Church "as soon as possible, and when doubts arise, say only, 'I believe, Lord. Help my unbelief.'"[20] Such directness may be abhorrent to the present generation given Elizabeth's grief and loneliness. But seen through the evangelical lens, it is simply an act of charity.

After St. Augustine lost his faith as an adolescent, his saintly mother was beside herself. Again and again, she confronted him, going so far on occasion as to shut him out of the house. Again and again, he spurned her entreaties. Had Monica known early in the life of her son what we know today – that her tears, prayers, and pressure would be instrumental in his ascent to sanctity (something she eventually witnessed) – her task would have been easier. For Augustine, as for most reverts, the journey home took many years, and along the way, there were others like Monica who used what critics might describe as "force." Once, when Augustine spoke cynically about the Faith at the bedside of a dying friend, the friend asked him to leave. Such a request could not have been easy under such circumstances, but it may well have helped one of the world's most brilliant intellectuals to come to his senses.

We mentioned earlier that Francis of Assisi risked his life to cross enemy lines in time of war to preach to Al-Kamil of Egypt. After instructing the sultan for a full two weeks, he gave him a choice: convert or suffer the loss of his soul.[21] Accounts differ on whether Al-Kamil was ever received into the Church. One thing, however, is certain, Francis won permission for his Friars Minor to evangelize the Sultan's entire realm.

Filippo Filicchi, Bishop Cheverus, and Francis of Assisi – all three were high-pressure salesmen. Then there is Francis Xavier, arguably the greatest of all missionaries, who served notice on the people of India, after preaching to them at length, that they must convert or suffer damnation. Tens of thousands chose baptism. In Japan, where he encountered widespread sodomy and divorce, along with polygamy and polytheism, he condemned all four, and within fifty years the Land of the Rising Sun was well its way to becoming Catholic. Later on, the Japanese would apostatize, but not for reasons having anything to do with Francis' methods.

If my readers are surprised to find that two saints by the name of Francis told their listeners to choose between Catholicism and the loss of their souls, they shouldn't be, since this was the choice given to Jewish leaders by Jesus, as well as the one given by the apostles to those who heard them preach (e.g. Acts 13:46-49). Our Lord told His seventy-two disciples, when He sent them out, that it would be easier for the people of Sodom on Judgment Day than for those who refused to give them a hearing.[22] Several years ago, New York subway cars featured an ad by a job placement firm that read, "If you're really good, you should always be looking." Just so. If people are what they ought to be, they will search out the truth and, on finding it, embrace it at any cost. In the words of John Paul II's *Redemptoris Missio* (1990), all men without exception have an "obligation to seek the truth, above all religious truth ... [and] hold to the truth once it is known."

The argument is sometimes made that conversion requires grace from on high. It surely does. But such grace is always on tap! Augustine, who is known as the "doctor of grace," taught what the Church has always taught: that God's enabling power is never denied to the earnest seeker.[23] If it were not so, why would Jesus have demanded conversion? The Gospel message was "repent and believe," not "repent and, *if possible*, believe." The appointment calendar of a dental hygienist may be filled months in advance. But not so with the Holy Spirit. The third person of the Blessed Trinity is available 24/7. No matter that one's livelihood, along with one's inheritance, could be imperiled by a change in religion, as is often the case. Given the sustaining power of Divine Providence, it is hard to justify the postponement. Legitimate excuses for making God wait are few and far between. Christ waits for each of us with open arms, and, as mentioned earlier, He wishes all men to come to the truth (1 Tim. 2:4).

MEDIA MISCHIEF

A media such as ours that is overwhelmingly anti-religious affects the soul of a nation the way a virus affects the body. Every one of the myths examined thus far is "in the air," so to speak. And this is not surprising. As mentioned earlier, St. Paul identified Satan as "the prince of the air" (Eph. 2:2). Most modern films are seamy, the songs are steamy, and the moral tone of novels has reached an all-time low. So pervasive is the rot that it leaves nothing untouched, including the world of classical music and art. Subversion is more subtle in the world of high culture than it is on the street, but it exists.

Recently, I attended a concert featuring music by Johannes Brahms and Robert Schumann, and glancing over the program notes, I came across an unflattering description of Brahms' relationship with Schumann's wife. I was astonished, knowing Brahms to be a deeply religious Lutheran. Based on what I've read, there is no hard evidence for adultery, or even flirtatious behavior. But evidence or no evidence, the movers and shakers of the secular media will stop at nothing to popularize the idea that loose morals are compatible with creative genius. They will do whatever it takes to conceal the linkage between time-tested artistic accomplishment and closeness to God.

Lest you think this an isolated incident, I attended an exhibit of Rembrandt paintings not long ago at the Detroit Institute of Arts. Strolling through the gallery and reading the captions beside each of the masterpieces, I was struck by the amount of attention given to the painter's affair with a house-keeper. Most visitors to the museum, knowing little about Rembrandt, would have concluded, on the basis of the curatorial prompts, that one can be immoral and, at the same time, a world-class painter. The fact is that Holland's master of light and darkness did his best work during periods when he was morally upright. When he fell from grace, his art suffered appreciably – so much so that a practiced eye, surveying practically any canvass, can tell the age of the artist and what was happening in his personal life at the time when he painted it. Exhibit attendees were doubly duped by the lack of any reference to Rembrandt's penchant for painting religious scenes. Few would have guessed that, as a Dutch Calvinist without ecclesiastical patronage and handicapped by the Protestant animus against "graven images," he produced far more religious art than any of his peers.

One can go further. A recent Metropolitan Museum of Art exhibit featuring likenesses of the writer Victor Hugo billed him as an atheist even though he loved the Bible, quoted from it often, and contributed to France's post-revolutionary restoration of Notre Dame Cathedral! The author of *Les Miserables* may have missed Sunday Mass. But since when does non-attendance at church make a person a non-believer?

Attend a Metropolitan Opera performance of *Rigoletto, Il Travatore,* or *La Traviata,* and, chances are, you will be handed a program describing the composer, Giuseppe Verdi, as an atheist whereas, like Hugo, he simply stayed home on Sunday at a certain time in his life. Something else likely to be included in the program notes is a reference to Verdi's cohabitation, without reference to the fact that he was a widower who had just suffered the catastrophic loss of his entire family. You will not read

that the gifted soprano with whom Verdi cohabited was unmar-
riageable by the standards of the day, owing to her checkered
past, or that Verdi eventually married her – the two remained
loyal for the rest of their lives. We are left with the impression,
once again, that a great composer was grossly immoral. In truth,
Verdi was a *fairly great* composer who was *somewhat religious*, as
compared with those who were *really great* and *really religious*
(e.g. Mozart, Beethoven, Haydn, Bach, Brahms, and Dvorak).

In any world other than that of leftist fiction, beauty is
inseparable from virtue. Writers such as Tolstoy and Ibsen may
have sowed their wild oats when they were young. But they did
not harness their God-given talent until they changed course
spiritually. *Anna Karenina* and *Hedda Gabler* were not the fruit
of dissipation. Artistic creativity of the highest order is incom-
patible with promiscuity.

One last example of media mischief: nearly every time
Mozart's opera *The Magic Flute* is performed in New York, the
audience learns that the opera has Masonic themes and that
Mozart was a Mason. It's no secret that the Pope has censured
Masonry. Ticket holders are thus led to the conclusion that the
most popular classical music composer of all time was a non-
practicing Catholic. No one would know from the program
notes that Austrian Masonry, unlike that in Spain, Italy, and
Latin America, was not anti-Catholic in Mozart's day or that the
Austrian bishops did not regard the papal censure as applicable
to their dioceses. Nowhere in the notes will it be indicated that
Mozart frequented Mass and confession with his fiancée, that he
composed a Mass for his wedding, or that, at the age of twenty-
two, he celebrated the success of a concert by praying the rosary.
Broadway and Hollywood productions of *Amadeus* that portray
him as foul-mouthed and ill-mannered fly in the face of his

real-life reputation, which was that of a gentleman. Wouldn't it be nice if the public prints informed us, every so often, that all of the greatest creative geniuses – men and women whose work has stood the test of time in such fields as art, literature, architecture, exploration, science, and statesmanship – have been exceptionally close to God?[25] It is a powerful argument for religion.

A "NARROW GATE" CHURCH

The same evangelist who dubbed Satan "the prince of the air" described the relationship of the Church to the world as one of crucifixion – Christians to the world and the world to Christians.[26] Paul may not have known it at the time, but he was putting his finger on one of the greatest challenges facing the Catholic evangelist: the fact that the Church expects so much of us. Low-church Protestants may ban dancing, theater, alcoholic beverages, and caffeine. But the things Catholicism proscribes are of far greater magnitude and, to a large extent, Bible-based: remarriage after divorce, euthanasia, same-sex "marriage," contraception, abortion, and in-vitro fertilization. Catholics who commit mortal sin must go down on their knees before a priest in confession. They must fulfill the weekly Mass requirement and embrace mystery. In an age that swears by science, they must believe in transubstantiation and papal infallibility on matters of faith and morals, not to mention the dogma of eternal damnation. For potential converts, these are hard pills to swallow. C. S. Lewis once wrote, in reference to hell, that "there is no doctrine which I would more willingly remove from Christianity than this, if it lay within my power."[27] Jehovah's Witnesses, Mormons, New Agers, and Hindus reject the concept altogether, while others circumvent it by holding that once one accepts Jesus as Lord and Savior, there is nothing to fear.

If the odds against becoming Christian are great, the odds against becoming Catholic are even greater. Jehovah's Witnesses and Quakers promise draft exemption, while Mormons have a well-earned reputation for taking care of their poor and elderly. Many churches offer fellowship based on social homogeneity. All the Catholic Church offers is the unvarnished truth, along with the persecution that invariably accompanies it. Its members will be called "imbeciles," bigots," "homophobes," "reactionaries," "servile," and "papists" (or "Romanists). According to the rubrics in use when I was confirmed, the presiding bishop gave me a slap on the face, suggesting the kind of reception I could expect from the world once I enlisted in the army of the Lord. Regretfully, this is no longer part of the rite, because it was inspiring, as well as instructive. Over a half-century ago, Bishop Fulton J. Sheen remarked famously that, "There are not a hundred people in America who hate the Catholic Church. There are millions who hate what they wrongly perceive the Catholic Church to be – which, of course, is quite a different thing." Today, there are millions of people who despise the Catholic Church for its fidelity to the apostolic code of faith and morals. Times have changed.

SCRIPTURAL SKEPTICISM

Last on our list of hurdles in the way of non-believers seeking the truth is the notion that the Gospel accounts are unreliable.[28] Allegations of error and contradiction were refuted many times over by theologians of the caliber of Tertullian,

Origen, Eusebius, Jerome, and Augustine. But the Scriptural skepticism of the 300s and 400s, like so many other heresies that should be long dead and gone, went underground and resurfaced centuries later in German academic circles. From there, it migrated to America, where it eventually found favor in Catholic seminaries and universities.

Every Sunday, readings from both the Old and New Testament are declared to be "the word of God," and God, by definition, cannot err or contradict himself. Nevertheless, post-Vatican II homilists caught up in an academic frenzy of disbelief were led to question authorship, order of Gospel composition, and accuracy of detail. Such preaching, highly dubious on scholastic grounds, was pedagogically disastrous, for by injecting cynicism into the mind of the average man, it undermined Bible study and apologetics – the twin pillars of public witness. Why read Scripture if one can't tell which verses are authentic? Why study apologetics if one can't quote the Bible with confidence?

The result of widespread uncertainty on the part of the American Church was an exodus of Catholics to Protestant denominations that know where they stand on Scripture and are thus more comfortable with Bible study and evangelization. A third to a half of all Evangelicals today are ex-Catholics! This is not to suggest that biblical concerns are the only reason for Catholic defection. But it would be a mistake, I should think, to rule out disenchantment with biblical skepticism as a factor in the current hemorrhage.

Such skepticism, which masquerades as "historical criticism," is neither historical nor critical in the sense of being open-minded and scientific. We will revisit it when we deal with the challenge of atheism. Suffice it to say for now that all the Fathers and Doctors of the Church have upheld the principle of biblical inerrancy. These men, who committed entire books of the Bible to memory, had a grasp of ancient culture that was vastly superior to our own since they were so much closer to it. Their access to works of history and commentary that have been lost to posterity (e.g., histories written by such authors as Orosius, Hegesippus, and Papias) is but one of many reasons to regard their work as authoritative.

The proceedings of the Second Vatican Council are instructive in this regard. When a handful of delegates sought to limit the principle of biblical inerrancy to matters of faith and morals, the motion was put to a vote and decisively *defeated*. Pope Paul VI intervened personally to ensure that nothing published by the Council so much as *hinted* at error or contradiction. When the Pontifical Biblical Council succumbed to skepticism, Paul demoted it, and John Paul II later faulted its members for unwarranted "conjectures" and a failure to "treat the Sacred Writings inspired by God" with proper "veneration."[29]

There may have been scholars who felt that biblical skepticism would undermine Protestant belief in *sola scriptura* (Scripture alone as the basis for truth). But this is not what happened. In 1982, Gleason Archer came out with his *New International Encyclopedia of Bible Difficulties*, one the best defenses of Scriptural inerrancy ever written. Allowing for the few instances in which Gleason writes as a Protestant, his work is as useful for Catholics as it is for those of other persuasions. Three years after Archer published his encyclopedia, Rev. William Most, a Catholic professor of classics and theology at Loras College, brought out *Free from All Error*, a brilliant defense of traditional teaching on inerrancy. But sadly, by the time Gleason and Most published their studies, practically all of our seminaries and universities were in the hands of skeptics, and the mind of the man in the pew had been poisoned.

It is easy to become discouraged considering the multitude of forces arrayed against us! But be of good cheer. In chapter 5, we shall begin dissecting God's word, and when we do, the emphasis will shift to something that is nothing if not heartening. Those who take to the street armed with Scripture (St. Paul's "sword of the spirit"), have every reason to believe, as did Julia Ward Howe when she wrote her Battle Hymn of the Republic, that God's truth goes "marching on."

CHAPTER 5

TAKING TO THE STREET

Mother Angelica, the greatest televangelist of the 20th century, once said, "Give me ten Jehovah's Witness-type Catholics and I can change the world."[1] In the chapters that follow, I will suggest what it takes to be one of Angelica's ten. First, though, a word about the woman herself, since she is without peer as a bearer of the Good News.

Not long after relocating from Canton, Ohio to Birmingham, Alabama, the future foundress of EWTN began discussing God's Word with her fellow nuns. Invited by Protestant friends to lead a Lenten Bible study, she agreed, and her course ran for five years, with Methodists, Baptists, and Episcopalians in attendance, along with Catholics. It was a life-changing experience. Soon she was turning out scores of Bible-based mini-books and founding the Catholic Family Missionary Alliance – eight thousand members strong – to disseminate her writings free of charge. The success of her first radio program, entitled "Journeys into Scripture," gave her added confidence, and once more, the experience was seminal because it was with Bible in hand and proof texts at the ready that she would captivate millions on a television network that John Paul II called "the key to restoring Catholicism in America." Scripture was her stock in trade, and she used it to great advantage in defense of the Faith. As of this writing, EWTN reaches 250 million homes in 104 countries.

Another name for defense of the Faith is apologetics, and if Angelica was supremely gifted as an apologist, so, too, was her predecessor on the airwaves, Bishop Fulton Sheen, dubbed by *Time* magazine "the golden-voiced Monsignor ... Catholicism's famed proselytizer ... America's first televangelist." Sheen's celebrated 1950s TV program, *Life Is Worth Living*, appealed to Americans of every persuasion and was beloved by millions. And what is interesting from an evangelical standpoint is that early in his teaching career, Sheen was appointed to the Apologetics chair at Catholic University.

Another way of putting it is that Scripture-driven apologetics is the common denominator of the Church's greatest televangelists and convert-makers. We can't all be like Mother Angelica or Fulton Sheen. But one thing all of us, without exception, *can* do is acquaint ourselves with the basic tools and techniques used in the defense of the Faith, beginning with the proof texts found in Appendix A of this book. For handy reference, subjects are listed in alphabetical order, and once readers are familiar with the responses suggested for each of the standard queries, they can forget about memorization.

Personally, I have a memory like a sieve. And so, when the need arises, I simply whip out a few 8x11 sheets of paper (Appendix A). With these in hand, I am fully equipped. Step #2 is to mold the contents of Appendix A into a persuasive sales pitch. For me, the unique selling point of the Church of Rome is its conformity to all of the biblical specifications laid down by Christ for His Church. And so I use it every day on the street when engaging Protestants, and when asked what I mean by specifications, I'm more than happy to oblige.

SPECIFICATION #1:
THE PAPACY

If there is anything that identifies Catholicism as the one true Church, it is Christ's commissioning of Peter to lead His followers.[2] Jesus entrusted the "keys" of the kingdom to one man alone, telling him that whatever he bound on earth would be bound in heaven. Peter was likewise the only apostle instructed by Our Lord to feed his sheep.[3] Under Peter, in order of authority, were the other apostles and then the seventy-two disciples. This pyramidal, one-man-on-top paradigm retained by the Catholic Church is its most distinguishing feature and the key to its unity.

The case for conformity to specification comes into even sharper focus when one recalls that, in establishing the papacy, Jesus was simply preserving a divinely ordained institution – one that had served the Chosen People for over a thousand years. The Jewish high priest, like the pope, was the supreme arbiter in matters of faith and morals – to the point of wielding life-and-death power over heretics. Jesus knew that the traditional Jewish office of high priest would pass out of existence in 70 A.D., the year Roman armies destroyed the Temple and, along with it, the genealogical records on which the entire priesthood was based as every priest was required to prove lineal descent from Aaron.

There are, of course, other reasons aside from Jewish tradition for believing that the power given to Peter was transferred to his successors as head of the Church. Why, first of all, would Our Lord limit the man-on-top paradigm to a single generation, knowing that the disunity which it was designed to prevent would be less of a problem for Peter than for those who came after? Secondly, when Christ vested the Fisherman with plenary power, He echoed, nearly verbatim, the words used to commission King Hezekiah's steward, Eliakim.[4] Stewardship was a permanent fixture of Jewish life, and Eliakim, like the pope, was expected to be a father to his people. Given the fact that the governing authority he wielded was second only to that of the monarch, there is but one conclusion; what Hezekiah intended on the level of statecraft, Jesus intended on a higher, spiritual level.

Protestants maintain that there is little historical evidence for the early exercise of papal authority. This is true. The paper trail left by a heavily persecuted Church is virtually nil, but what evidence there is supports Catholic claims. When dissension broke out in the church of Corinth in 95 A.D., Pope Clement, the fourth bishop of Rome, sent a letter to the Corinthians that is unmistakably papal in tone:

> We have been somewhat tardy in giving heed to the matters of dispute that have arisen among you … . Dearly beloved, we write not only as admonishing you … [Our Apostles knew] there would be strife over the bishop's office … *They appointed* [persons] *and provided a continuance* … . It is shameful conduct in Christ that it should be reported that the very steadfast and ancient Church of the Corinthians, for the sake of one or two persons, maketh sedition against its presbyters … Let us therefore root this out quickly … Learn to submit yourselves unto the presbyters and receive the chastisement unto repentance … But if certain persons should be disobedient unto the words *spoken by Him* [i.e., the Holy Spirit] *through us* let them understand that they will entangle themselves in no slight transgression and danger … . [italics added for emphasis].

If anyone was well situated morally, as well as geographically, to act as arbiter for the church of Corinth it was Christ's "beloved disciple," John. Yet it is Clement who intervenes. And whether or not his opinion was requested, it was heeded and read aloud by Corinthian lectors for centuries.

SPECIFICATION #2:
UNITY

Another specification contained in Scripture that can be used to identify the true Church of Christ is religious unity. Our Lord prayed for it, predicted it ("there shall be one fold, one shepherd"), and guaranteed it by putting one man in charge of His flock and sending the Holy Spirit to lead it to the fullness of truth.[5] Bishop Ignatius of Antioch, in a letter to John's pupil, Polycarp of Smyrna, called unity "the greatest of all goods," and we know that his co-religionists were blessed with it because they are described as being "of one mind."[6]

Today, there is only one church distinguished for unity of the kind enjoyed by the early Christians – Catholicism. As an organization that is both human and divine, it may have dissenters within its ranks, but it doesn't suffer from the division and sectarianism condemned by Peter and Paul.[7] Our separated brethren, without a comprehensive catechism or a court of last appeal on dogma, differ on everything from artificial birth control to the meaning of the Eucharist, which is why they continue to splinter.

SPECIFICATION#3:
THE REAL PRESENCE

Belief in the Real Presence of Jesus in Holy Communion is a third example of Catholic conformity to biblical specifications.

Jesus told His followers that, "unless you eat the flesh of the Son of Man and drink His blood, you shall not have life in you … for My flesh is food indeed and My blood is drink indeed" (John 6:51-57). This came after the miraculous multiplication of loaves (verses 1-15), and many of Jesus' followers, upon hearing it, wanted out. "This is a hard saying!" they told Him (John 6:61). But Jesus stood his ground, refusing to qualify his language. "Does this scandalize you?" He asked, comparing the Eucharist to the miracle of his Ascension (John 6:63). After repeating himself three times, He let the protesters go, and as far as we know, they never returned (verses 61-67). How likely is it that the world's greatest teacher would let "many" of his disciples go on the basis of a simple misunderstanding – one that could have been eliminated with the utterance of four words, "Don't take me literally." Notice, too, that the problem was not one of misunderstanding. Rather, as John points out, it was one of belief (verses 65 and 70). They could not or would not *believe*. People still refuse to believe!

Those who deny the Real Presence of Christ in the Eucharist should reread John 6, paying particular attention to verses 63-64, wherein Jesus warns that the Eucharist cannot be understood except through the medium of the "spirit." Those who were of the flesh took Jesus' words as a reference to cannibalism because they couldn't or wouldn't believe the God-Man capable of giving His flesh and blood without being, in any way, diminished. Paul, in his first letter to the Corinthians, put his finger on the underlying problem, "The sensual man does not perceive the things that are of God."[8]

It is unlikely that the apostles grasped the meaning of the Eucharist at this point, or even when Jesus lifted bread at the Last Supper and said, "This is my body." To be sure, He used the verb *"is"* when He might well have said, "this *represents* my body" or "this *means* my body." Nevertheless, it is doubtful that His followers understood Him fully until after the Resurrection. The first indication of apostolic recognition comes when Paul tells the Corinthians that anyone who eats the consecrated bread unworthily "without distinguishing the body eats and drinks judgment to himself" (1 Cor. 11:29). Next on record is the testimony of Ignatius, martyred bishop of Antioch and a contemporary of John (d. circa 110 A.D.) who had the following to say about the reason some of his Christian followers were abstaining from Holy Communion: "They do not confess that the Eucharist is the Flesh of Our Savior Jesus Christ." Such people, he mentioned, should be shunned (Letter to the Smyrneans). Another example of early Christian discrimination!

SPECIFICATION #4:
CLERICAL CELIBACY AND POVERTY

Jesus encouraged the leaders of the early Church to do two things highly unusual for anyone raised in a Jewish culture. First, they were to embrace celibacy; "Let him accept it who can," He told them.[9] Secondly, they were to heed His advice to the rich young man: "If you wish to be perfect, sell what you have and … come, follow me."[10]

The apostles strove to live in accord with their Master's wishes, and we can see that here again, members of Catholic religious orders, along with the vast majority of priests, bear the biblical imprint. We know that Peter was married. But he is the exception that proves the rule, because when he played host to Jesus, the meal was served by his mother-in-law. If his wife had been present, she would have been the one serving.

Was he a widower when Jesus called him to the priesthood? Was he separated from his spouse? One cannot say with any degree of certainty. But this much is clear: all of the apostles, including Peter, renounced family life, embraced poverty (by holding all things in common), and relied for their sustenance on a common fund, making themselves available for any task, however dangerous, the Lord might call upon them to undertake.

Christian celibacy is particularly striking in light of the fact that all Jews except the Scribes were expected to marry, an expectation that explains why so many second and third generation priests had wives. Christian communities sprang up rapidly, they needed pastors, and those chosen for ordination had to be on the older side because it was the custom for elders, and elders alone, to take the lead. Since virtually every elder among the Jews was married, there was no alternative to a married clergy. But – and this is a huge "but" – the latest scholarship indicates that married priests were expected to live with their wives as brother and sister.

As an aside, modern day Eastern Rite churches in union with Rome allow their clergy to marry. But in deference to the wishes of Our Lord, there are no married bishops, and priests can't marry after ordination. Likewise, in the case of Greek and Russian Orthodox congregations that operate independently of Rome there is no married episcopacy. In sum, all Christian communities with the exception of those that are Protestant have honored Christ's preference for celibate leadership. Catholicism is unique, though, in terms of the extent to which the honor goes.

SPECIFICATION #5:
PERSECUTION

"No servant is greater than his master," said Jesus, "if they persecute me, they will persecute you ... If they do this when the wood is green, what will happen when it is dry?"[11] No religious founder suffered as Jesus did, and no religious body has suffered as much as the Catholic Church.

Under the Roman imperium, Christians (i.e., Catholics) endured torture so frightful that one can scarcely bear to read about it. And it is not just what happened under such emperors as Domitian, Aurelius, Decius, and Diocletian. Many years later, post-Reformation rulers in Britain and Scandinavia were brutal. Even today in the United States, no church is more disdained, more hated, or more feared than the Church of Rome. Hitler, Stalin, and Mao did their best to wipe Catholicism off the map. During World War II in Holland, the Nazis rounded up and gassed all Dutch Jews who had converted to Catholicism, while passing over Protestants of Jewish ancestry. Anglicans have never been persecuted in countries with a long Anglican history; Lutherans have yet to suffer in countries that are predominately Lutheran. Catholics, on the other hand, have paid the price of discipleship everywhere, even in countries that are overwhelmingly Catholic. One has but to recall the enormities of France's Robespierre, Mexico's Calles, and the Spanish Republicans of the 1930s.

ADDITIONAL SPECIFICATIONS

There are many other specifications that identify Catholicism as "the church of Christ" – or, in words our Protestant

brethren would understand, "the Bible church." Among them
are the following:

1.   Both the Old and the New Testaments require attendance
     at weekly assembly (Lev. 23:2-3; Heb. 10:25). So does the
     Catholic Church.

2.   The first Christians anointed with oil those who were
     seriously ill and prayed over them (James 5:14-15). The
     Catholic Church does this when it administers the Last
     Rites.

3.   Christ prohibited remarriage after divorce, and once again,
     Catholicism follows suit. We will treat this subject more
     fully in chapter 7.

4.   The New Testament contains references to bishops, as well
     as priests (elders) and deacons. The Catholic Church has
     all three levels of ordination.

5.   The early Church was a church of miracles, with a prom-
     ise of miracles to come. The Catholic Church is likewise a
     church of miracles – those, most notably, that occurred at
     Guadalupe, Lourdes, and Fatima.

6.   The early Church was a church that believed in the power
     of relics. In the New Testament, cures are obtained by
     touching the clothing of a saint (Acts 19:12). In the Old,
     a corpse is restored to life after being brought into contact
     with the bones of a prophet (2 Kings 13:21). The Catholic
     Church retains this age-old belief in the power of relics.

7.   Jesus told His followers to go into all the world and tell the
     good news (Mark 16:15). The Catholic Church is more
     universal – i.e., more Catholic – than any other Christian
     body. At last count, Mass in Los Angeles was being cel-
     ebrated in 53 languages.

8. The Church is closer in moral values to early Christianity than any other Christian body, holding fast to the apostolic ban on abortion and contraception.

9. The Catholic Church of today and the Church of the Apostles are identical in terms of democratic ethos. In the words of St. Paul, there were "not many wise according to the flesh" in the Church of his time, "not many mighty, not many noble. But the foolish things of the world, Paul says, have been chosen by God to put to shame the [so-called] 'wise'" (1 Cor. 1:26-27). Enter a Catholic church today almost anywhere in the world, and you will find the same social mix: chambermaids and firemen in the same pew with attorneys and physicians.

10. Jesus urged His disciples to strive for perfection, and the Church has produced more souls that answer to this description (i.e., more saints) than any other Christian church.

11. Something as incidental as the practice of kneeling at Mass is also Scriptural. The one description given by the Gospels of Jesus' praying posture has Him kneeling (Luke 22:45). Likewise in the case of Peter and Paul (Acts 9:40; 20:36; 21:5). Psalm 95 bids us "kneel before the Lord who made us," and we have it from Isaiah: "Unto me [the Lord] every knee shall bend." (Isaiah 45:23 – Jerusalem Bible). Eusebius, in describing James, son of Alphaeus and the first bishop of Jerusalem, tells us that his knees were as calloused as those of a camel from kneeling in prayer (see William Barclay's commentary on the letters of James and Peter, pp. 12-13; also Phil. 2:10).

12. One of the first things Jesus did following the Resurrection was to give His apostles the power to forgive sins. "Whose

sins you forgive," He told them, "they are forgiven. Whose sins you retain [i.e., refuse to absolve] are retained." The Catholic Church is one of the few Christian bodies that acts on this commission.

13. Jesus had an all-male priesthood. So does the Church. Our Lord infuriated Jewish leaders by curing on the Sabbath. He endorsed foods regarded as unclean. He dispensed with the ritual washing of hands. He talked with a Samaritan, and a woman at that. In short, He could have recruited women for the priesthood if He had so desired because He was not bound by Jewish culture – priestesses were common in Greece, Rome, and Egypt. His ordination of an all-male priesthood was deliberate, and the Catholic Church has acted accordingly.

14. Jesus conversed with Old Testament saints Moses and Elijah on the Mount of Transfiguration. He also told a parable in which a man in purgatory, anxious for the salvation of family members and seeking to be of service, prays to Abraham for a favor (Luke 16:24). Scripture enjoins us to pray for one another, and oftentimes, we ask our friends for help. If we can ask our friends who are alive to intercede for us, why not those who are dead – especially the saints who have connections? The Catholic Church is, once again, in line with Scripture.

15. Judging from the Book of Revelation, Mary was highly venerated by the early Church, and this is how Catholics have always regarded her. John pictures her as clothed with the sun and wearing a crown of twelve stars (Rev. 12). The only other person described by the Bible as clothed with the sun is God Himself. As for the crown, it suggests a role similar to that of the queen mother, who was second only

to the Jewish king in importance. Jesus, on the Cross at Calvary, went so far as to tell John, His favorite apostle, to regard Mary as his mother – "Son, behold your mother," "Woman, behold your son." Recall, too, that John's biological mother, Salome, was looking on at the time. If Mary was John's mother spiritually, she was, by extension, the mother of *all* the apostles and indeed of all Christians. In Revelation 12, John calls her the mother of all who witness to Jesus and keep the Commandments. Some commentators view John's "woman" as a reference to the Church. But how can this be? The "woman" in question is described as giving birth to a son who will rule all nations with an iron rod – clearly Jesus. How, then, can John's "woman" mean the Church when it was not the Church that gave birth to Jesus, but rather Jesus who gave birth to the Church?

16. Jesus and His apostles favored a Bible that contained the deuterocanonical (or apocryphal) books (i.e., the Greek version of Hebrew Scripture known as the Septuagint). We know this because eighty percent of the references to the Old Testament found in the New Testament are taken from the Septuagint. Catholic bibles have always included the deuterocanonical books.

SUMMARY

Are there Christian churches other than the Church of Rome that conform to some of the above-mentioned specifications? Yes. But the Catholic Church is the only one that conforms to *all* of them. Furthermore, there are many self-described "Christian" churches that not only fail to conform but stand in stark opposition to one or more of Jesus' specifications.

As an aside, practices such as praying the rosary and granting indulgences are nowhere to be found in the Bible. But the Bible doesn't list all the practices of the early Church. Even if it did, the Church, like a family, is a living organism. It grows over time, and as it grows, new practices are added. We do things in the Marks home that we didn't do twenty or thirty years ago. Nevertheless, who we are and what we believe as a family hasn't changed. A man looks and sounds very different at age twenty than he looked and sounded at the age of twenty weeks. Yet he is who he is. Although an oak tree is very different from an acorn, the two are essentially the same.

STREET SMARTS

Thus far, in our defense of the Faith, we have relied almost entirely on Bible-based arguments. Some of those, however, whom we meet on the street or at a cocktail party, will be totally ignorant of Scripture, and so one must be ready to improvise.

I shall never forget the day on the street when a motorcyclist in a black leather jacket pulled up on his Harley Davidson, raised his right hand, and said to me, "I don't need to go to church; I have God right here," pointing to his chest. I could have cited Leviticus 23:2-3, along with Hebrews 10:25. But there was something about the man's bearing that seemed to call for a less formal response. "You've got God in your heart?" I asked. "Terrific! You're blessed!" He smiled and went on, "I've been off alcohol for thirty years and helped others kick the habit. I survived a life-threatening gallbladder operation. I'm a happy man!" Answering again I said, "You're twice blessed! I'll give you an 'A' for happiness. But you want to know something?

There'd be a plus next to the 'A' if you became a serious Catholic, and your 'A+' would stand up under life's heaviest body blows."

The man's willingness to listen kept on beckoning and so I continued. "If your parents invited you to dinner once a week, would you stand them up?" After hesitating a moment, he answered, "No." This was all I needed to press on, "As Catholics, we believe that our heavenly Father invites us, indeed requires us, to attend His dinner party once a week. Are you familiar with Sacred Scripture, which requires weekly assembly?" He looked at me benignly, and so I offered him a tract on the reliability of Scripture, which he took – "Just some food for thought," I said. "It's been great talking with you. My name is Fred. What's yours?" Before revving up his motorcycle, we exchanged contact information, and I said a prayer of thanksgiving. The Holy Spirit had given me a window of opportunity.

On another occasion, while I was speaking in Washington Square Park for the Catholic Evidence Guild, a man came up to me, identified himself as a homosexual, and asked why the Church condemns sodomy. "Do you believe in the Bible as the word of God?" I queried. His negative response was what I expected. Had it been otherwise, I could have pointed out that the Old Testament, as well as the New, outlaws sexual intercourse between members of the same-sex. In the Book of Genesis, God strikes Onan dead for wasting his seed (not, as some have argued, for refusing to raise up issue to his dead brother). Later, in the same book, God punishes unnatural lust by raining fire and brimstone on Sodom and Gomorrah, and the enormity of the offense is clear from the fact that Sodomites are the only sinners other than the fallen angels known to be in hell.[12] Leviticus and Deuteronomy are equally condemnatory, as is the stance taken by Paul: those who engage in same-sex geni-tal activity are deserving of death.[13]

These arguments were of no use to me, of course, in dealing with a man who identified himself as gay. So I tried to state the Catholic position in terms he could understand. "How highly do you value human life?" I began. He looked at me blankly, and so I went on, "If you had a daughter, and she was taken from you, how much ransom would you put up for a safe return? If she were mine, there'd be no limit to what I would sacrifice, even if it meant my home and all of my life's savings. If today you yourself, a perfect stranger, were to fall into deep water without knowing how to swim, I would risk my life to save you. This is what we mean, as Catholics, when we say that human life is sacred."

He had nothing to say, as expected, and so I told him that since we regard the life of every individual as sacred, we view the procreative act the same way, along with marriage, the institution that protects human life. "And this," I continued, "is why we oppose divorce and remarriage, along with contra-ception, abortion, and euthanasia." On a roll, I proceeded to put the crowning touch on my argument: "You have no idea of the happiness that results from a belief in the sacredness of life. Avoidance of AIDS isn't the half of it." To my surprise, the man was *still* speechless. So I offered him a tract on the reliability of Scripture. He took it before walking slowly away, and to this day, I have no idea whether any of my words hit home. But it matters not. The Lord grades on effort, not results, and I knew in my heart of hearts that I had done all that I could.

ANGER MANAGEMENT

In neither of the situations described above was I really under the gun. But anyone who's been on the street for any length of time knows what it's like to be on the receiving end of hissing, four-letter words, and the smell of liquor.

Once, when I was speaking for the Catholic Evidence Guild in one of the parks, a swordsman dressed in a Zorro cape and black mustache drew my listeners away by simply standing next to me and waving his weapon. He would toss an apple into the air, then cleave it in two on its way down. His audience was enthralled! What could I do except wait for an opportunity to engage him in conversation? When the hoped-for moment arrived, I steered our conversation onto the subject of extramarital sex. He seemed quite happy to chat! In the meantime, my fellow evangelists carried on. Such incidents are rare. But they go with the territory, and those who can't take the heat should get out of the kitchen.

I can think of at least two instances in which I behaved with less than perfect self-possession. Once, a skeptic queried me about biblical inerrancy. I offered him a tract on the subject, but he wouldn't take it. Instead, he asked me a question on medieval culture that I couldn't answer. So I shot back, "If you're not interested enough to read one of our tracts, I see no reason to go any further." End of conversation. Further discussion might have been fruitless, but I had no call to be dismissive, and I certainly shouldn't have been afraid to admit ignorance. No one has all the answers. My duty was simply to take down the man's contact information and get back to him.

In the second instance, a young man in his twenties came up to me one day and fired off a series of smart-aleck questions.

Instead of staying on message, I returned ridicule for ridicule. "Sophistry and sauciness are unworthy of a man of your intelligence. You're squandering your God-given talent." The exchange was over and I felt empty. However infuriated one may be, there is little to be gained by trading put-down for put-down. The goal of the apologist is to make the case for belief.

One of the first things one learns as a street evangelist is that one can't force a person to believe – you can lead a horse to water, but you can't make it drink. However persuasive we may be on an intellectual plane, we cannot win souls without winning hearts. In the words of Ben Franklin, "The mind changed against its will is of the same opinion still."

All exchanges with passersby should end as they began, on a note of camaraderie: "It was good talking with you today … a real privilege … thanks for lending us your ear and taking the time to share ideas … Come back and see us again."

This is not to say that one must be a doormat. In certain situations, forbearance can be as harmful as over-assertiveness, and Jesus, who did not suffer fools gladly, didn't recommend it: "Do not throw your pearls before swine."[14] Nevertheless, to show that we take seriously the Christian obligation to love our enemy, we must be patient and long-suffering. The prayer with which members of the Catholic Evidence Guild commence their meetings has this very end in view:

> St. Paul, help us in our work on the street corner to
> see in every aimless question, a human soul desperately
> grasping for the dignity of which it has been robbed;
> in every aggressive challenge, a human soul steeped in
> the conflict between this world and the next; in every
> angry denial, a human soul shrinking from the Sac-
> rifice of the Cross; in every false statement, a human
> soul misled by false prophets; in every scornful laugh,

a human soul deprived of the only Real Joy; in every listener, the image and likeness of God.

If your interlocutor won't listen for more than two seconds without interrupting, silence can speak volumes, especially when accompanied by a smile. It says, "Your pitch leaves me cold. I've heard it all before." You may find yourself on the receiving end of a long list of criticisms, in which case there is only one response, "I'd be happy to answer your questions, but I can't take them all at once. Let me know which ones are most important, and we'll go from there."

Folks who repeat themselves many times instead of responding to what you say may feel that any attempt to counter your argument would be futile. So they cover their ears. What I usually do in cases like this is recommend a good Catholic apologetics text such as Karl Keating's *Catholicism and Fundamentalism* or David Currie's *Born Fundamentalist, Born Again Catholic.* I tell them that I make a business of familiarizing myself with all kinds of anti-Catholic literature because I feel I owe it to my adversaries to know where they are coming from. And then I pop the question: Don't they regard themselves as under a similar obligation?

Some may hear you out and even thank you for what you've said. But bias dies hard. No one has ever gotten down on his knees before me and asked for baptism! Conversion is normally a long and arduous journey. Intellectual conviction can take years, and once convicted, the seeker must crank up enough gumption to face estrangement from relatives and friends, even loss of a job. Finally, he must make a Herculean effort to bring spouse and/or children on board.

The satisfaction of the evangelist has less to do with the number of converts he makes than in knowing that he has provided food for thought and helped folks take one or two steps forward on what could be a mile-long faith journey. I remember a convert on EWTN's *Journey Home* recalling something an evangelical Catholic told him on the streets of Buenos Aires when he was a boy. Though he wasn't aware of it at the time, it lodged deep in his subconscious, only to surface many years later and point him in the right direction.

DEALING WITH CHURCH SCANDAL

When folks bring up Church scandal, it is the better part of valor to level with them. Share your outrage and quote Jesus, "It were better for him if a millstone were hung about his neck and he were thrown into the sea than that he should cause one of these little ones to sin."[15] But once you have made your admission, be sure to point out that the percentage of Catholic clergy who are culpable is small in comparison with what obtained at the time of Christ when eight or nine percent of the apostolic band was rotten to the core (one out of twelve). Judas Iscariot, treasurer for the apostolic band and handpicked by Jesus, stole from the common purse and turned traitor. Yet Our Lord kept him on as treasurer to the very end, calling him "friend" in the Garden of Gethsemane moments before his betrayal. Equally to the point, Christ *predicted* future scandals, telling His followers that such incidents would be "impossible" to avoid.[16] It is safe to say that a church without scandal is not the Church of Christ.

Imagine an op-ed piece in a hypothetical "Jerusalem Times" the day after the Resurrection citing church scandal as proof of the hollowness of Christian claims and reminding readers of Jesus' observation, "You will know them by their fruits."[17] There will always be grist for the secular mill because Catholicism has a side that is profoundly human. All this proves, however, is that the Church is also divine. As Hilaire Belloc quipped, "No merely human institution run with such knavish imbecility would have lasted a fortnight."[18]

It is not often that the subject of media bias comes up on the street. But I will bring it up in order to make one thing very clear: when the secular press gives the mistaken impression that there is a disproportionate prevalence of sex abuse among the Catholic clergy, it is running true to form. Exhibit A is the annual March for Life in Washington, D.C., a predominantly Catholic event that attracts hundreds of thousands in weather that can be bitterly cold. Relatively few know about the March because, year in and year out, secular news outlets ignore it or relegate it to the back pages. I happened to be on a research project utilizing Jewish newspapers at the start of the millennium, and I can assure you, from what I read, that the rabbis left as much to be desired as their opposite numbers in the Church of Rome when it came to the sexual abuse of minors. Yet hardly anyone knew about it because it was not featured in the mainstream press.

ANSWERING APOSTATES

No group is harder to reach than ex-Catholics. Many, if not most, are wedded to a way of life that conflicts with what they learned growing up. They will not tell you that they've gone in for contraception, abortion, or remarriage after divorce. Typically, they try to score points on peripheral issues such as Church scandal. Many are as closed-minded as writer Graham Greene was when he met Padre Pio. Greene had adulterous liaisons with a half dozen women and frequented brothels. When, therefore, he witnessed the stigmata of Padre Pio, he declined to meet the holy man because he knew it would call for reformation. "I don't want to change my life by meeting a saint," he admitted (Scribner, *The Shadow of God*).

In dealing with hardness of heart and the blindness that invariably accompanies it, it's best to get to the point.[19] You might ask the people with whom you are talking, for example, how they stand on abortion. For those who accept Scripture as divinely inspired yet see nothing wrong with killing an unborn child, you can quote God's words to the prophet Jeremiah, "Before I formed you in the womb, I knew you."[20] The Almighty is actively engaged in forming the body and soul of every child from the moment of conception, and He is not a worker who wishes to be disturbed.

If apostates play the blame game – accusing a priest or nun of sins of commission or omission – grant that Catholics are human, like everyone else. Priests, bishops, cardinals, popes – *all* make mistakes. The thing to stress is that the Church, which dispenses life-giving grace through its sacraments, has never ceased to teach the truth in its fullness. For a model letter to a lapsed Catholic with whom you have found it difficult to exchange more than a few words, see Appendix E.

DEALING WITH CAFETERIA CATHOLICS

A large percentage of American Catholics are theologically deviant, and this is nothing new. Sixteen hundred years ago, St. Augustine spoke of having a "mob" of bad and false Catholics in his diocese.

In today's American Church, there is little difference, apart from nomenclature, between apostates and cafeteria Catholics.

Those who support abortion, contraception, remarriage after divorce, or same-sex "marriage" are flying in the face of papal teaching authority, the defining tenet of our faith. They may not have left the Church, but they are as good as gone because if the Church, which claims infallibility on faith and morals, is wrong in this matter, it is a sham. Likewise in the case of the Eucharist. Either the Magisterium is right on Transubstantiation, or the Mass is blasphemous.

Cafeteria Catholics need to be reminded of the basis for the Church's authority (Matt. 16:18-19) and urged to check out the reasoning behind what it teaches. They may think they are serious, but the litmus test is whether they are willing to make a *bona fide* effort to get to the bottom of the whys and wherefores.

CHAPTER 6

THE APPROACH TO ATHEISTS, MUSLIMS AND JEWS

There are Protestants who believe that in order to be saved one must be Christian. Some warn that unless you join their sect you will be damned. This, however, is not the Catholic position. The Church of Rome has always held that disbelief resulting from invincible ignorance – i.e. misinformation, lack of information, or a psychological block – is excusable.[1]

There are people in distant parts of the world who have never met a Christian. They may know next to nothing about Christianity, let alone Catholicism. There are also Christians not of our persuasion who have yet to read the life of a single saint or make the acquaintance of a single virtuous, well-informed Catholic. Some have had parents who filled them with hatred for "the whore of Babylon." Ask them if they know the story of Lourdes or Fatima and they draw a blank. Few have the vaguest idea of the Church's contribution to western civilization. Peter and Paul assure us that such people can be saved if they follow the Natural Law and live by the light of their conscience.[2]

To be sure, there is less excuse nowadays than there once was for ignorance of Christ and his Church because most bookstores carry the Bible, and if they don't, they can order it. More people than ever before know how to read, and the resources on the Internet are vast.

This said, pagans are as much God's children as anyone else, and so it stands to reason that He wants for them what He wants for all His sons and daughters. The same Jesus who said that no one could come to the Father except through Him (John 14:6) prophesied that the heathen Ninevites, along with the pagan Queen of Sheba, would rise on the last day to judge the living and the dead.[3] It is hard to imagine our Lord saving people who never heard of Him. But the grace by which non-Christians attain to goodness and conquer evil was won by His Passion. Why else would Abraham, Isaac, and Jacob be numbered "among the living"; why else would Jesus commend a Roman centurion for his "faith"?[4]

It is only natural to wonder why we should go out of our way and even risk our lives to bring the Good News to non-Catholics if there is salvation outside the Church. We do it because it is the will of Our Lord, who gave His precious blood that all might have the fullness of the truth. He would never have suffered and died on the Cross if Christianity didn't matter, and matter greatly. The truth sets us free, and so we want folks to have it.

ATHEISTS

I thank the atheists whom I meet on the street for taking the time to talk, because polite, good-natured sparring sharpens the mind and helps us tell truth from falsehood. I tell them, too, with a gleam in the eye, that we have one very important thing in common: an interest in religion. This helps to break the ice. Then I take the next step, which is to explain why I'm Christian and Catholic.

If you are ever in this position, you may find that before you have a chance to say very much, the atheist will bring up evolution because he assumes it gives the *coup de grace* to religion. But you can remind him that evolution, as a theory (which is all it is), has its critics, some of whom are Ph.D.s in science; also that Catholics are free to interpret Genesis metaphorically in a way that allows for evolution provided they recognize the following: (a) that God is the force behind the process; (b) that at some point along the line, He infused a human soul into the body of an animal; (c) that there was such a thing as Original Sin; (d) that this sin, on the part of a first set of parents, had the consequences recorded in Genesis.

A second query almost certain to come from atheists and other non-believers is how a good God can be responsible for natural disasters and devastating diseases. How can He create people who commit ghastly crimes? You can't refer an atheist to the Bible, but what you *can* do is suggest that there is a distinctly positive side to pain. If nothing else, it serves as a corrective to human pride. Ask you friend what he would be like without the humbling prospect of illness and death. Tell him you know what *you* would be like. When speaking with atheists who have no explanation for physical evil, ask them to call to mind the people in their lives who have been unusually kind. Then ask if these people who made a favorable impression on them are not the ones who have met with the most adversity. The lives of historical greats testify again and again to the value of suffering. One might add too, that as Catholics we have the consolation of knowing that God will never send us more trouble than we can handle (1 Cor. 10:13); also that we can offer up our suffering for a share in Christ's redemptive sacrifice (Col. 1:24).

If they bring up man's cruelty to his fellow man, you can explain that this is the fault of man, not God. If the Lord had created marionettes – if we were mere puppets on a string without the awesome power of free will – God could not love us as He does, nor could we love him in return.

Third on the atheist list of charges is the allegation that religion causes war. Like all falsehoods, this one contains a kernel of truth. There have been times when people fought for their faith. Judas Maccabeus took up arms in defense of Judaism. During the 1920s and 1930s, the Mexican Cristeros entered the lists for Catholicism. Things worth living for are worth fighting for! One can argue, though, that each of the above-mentioned wars was caused by *intolerance* of religion, rather than by religion itself. History reveals that men fight for all kinds of things, including self-aggrandizement, national honor, and political preferment. The United States has fought a dozen wars, but not one of them has had anything to do with religion. Ask your friends what they make of the fact that the least religious of all centuries, the twentieth, has produced more in the way of war, devastation, and cruelty than any other. Worth recalling, too, is what Jesus told fellow Jews bent on fighting the Romans: "Render to Caesar the things that are Caesar's." Had Our Lord's advice been heeded, Roman armies would never have destroyed Jerusalem and scattered the Jewish people to the ends of the earth.

If time permits, you can point out that over the centuries the Church brought warfare under control to a degree unheard of by today's standards. The medieval "Truce of God," which began by outlawing war on Sundays and religious feast days, was eventually extended to 285 days annually. There were safe havens for refugees (the "Peace of God"), along with a code of chivalry that required warriors to respect the rights of noncombatants, women, children, and pilgrims. Long intervals of peace are rare in any age, but Paris remained untouched by invasion or civil strife for five hundred years, enabling Christian civilization to take deep root in central France.

Most people you meet on the street are unaware that many of the so-called wars of religion were turf battles, with political motives uppermost in the minds of the combatants. The most important of the so-called "wars of religion," the Thirty Years' War (1618-1648), began with Catholics fighting Protestants who'd appropriated huge tracts of Church land. The conflict ended as a struggle between Catholic France and the Catholic Hapsburgs of Austria, with the pope accused of favoring the side allied with the Protestant Swedes. Even today, in many areas of the world where Muslims are fighting Christians, the quarrel has less to do with religion than with who controls Palestine and other parts of the Middle East.

If your atheist friends are still with you after you have dealt with the standard objections, it will be time to walk them through the classic, five-point brief for belief mentioned in Chapter 2 and repeated here for convenience: (1) Jesus claimed to be God; (2) He proved it by the miracles He worked, culminating in His Resurrection; (3) He established a Church; (4) Catholicism conforms to all the specifications laid down for it; (5) Scripture, upon which the first four points are based, is reliable.

For anyone outside the Christian perimeter, whether it be an atheist, agnostic, Hindu, Buddhist, Jew, or Muslim, five points are all you need to make the case for Catholicism. And because the first four are dependent on the fifth, your principal object is to demonstrate the inerrancy of God's word.

One way of doing this is to hold up a dollar bill and promise it to anyone who can come up with a single error or contradiction in Scripture aside from those that are due to miscopying or mistranslation – i.e. the ones that are easily recognized, easily corrected, and inconsequential. I've done this on numerous occasions and never known it to fail.

We have thousands of handwritten copies of the Gospels from all over the world, some of them dating back to the second and third centuries, and the discrepancies are so few that one can be certain of 99% of the text. As for the remaining 1%, it has no bearing on dogma. Out of a thousand biblical prophecies, no less than half have been borne out, while none have ever been disproven. Lastly, there isn't a single archaeological dig that has proven the Bible conclusively wrong, while scores of excavations have shown it to be accurate – down to the price of a slave at the time of Moses.

I will deal with this subject at greater length later in the upcoming section on Islam because Muslim objections are largely scriptural. But let me say, in advance, that it pays to have tracts on hand that make the case for scriptural inerrancy. Folks need to know that Jesus really did and said what He is thought to have done and said. Once you convince them of this, the rest is relatively easy.

TALKING WITH MUSLIMS

For those who face estrangement from relatives and friends if they renounce their religion, the road to Rome can be extremely difficult. Muslim converts, in particular, must be brave, because

Islam regards apostasy as a capital crime. Their very lives may be in danger. Still, there is reason for hope. St. Vincent Ferrer converted 8,000 Muslims in the southern, Islamic portion of Spain during the 14th century, and six hundred years later, a fair number of French Muslims joined the Church.

John Paul II, the first pope to enter a mosque, expressed "a high regard" for the Muslims. He admired their "religiosity" and was not the first of our faith to do so.[3] Blessed Charles de Foucauld (1858-1916), missionary to the semi-nomadic Tuaregs of Algeria, began life as a *bon vivant*. It was "wine, women, and song" until he traveled to North Africa and observed Muslims at prayer. The sheer intensity of their devotion gave him a sense for God's abiding presence, and from that time on, he chose belief over agnosticism, and asceticism over hedonism. Islam lifted his soul. It made him a better man. And so his story is a good one to share with Muslim friends.

It would be superfluous to add that all of us in the West have bitter memories of 9/11. The terror that triggered the Crusades continues to rankle, along with the knowledge that Muslim armies stood at the gates of Vienna after conquering Constantinople and much of Hungary. Muslim sailors came within a hair's breadth at Lepanto of winning control of the seas. As for the atrocities committed time and again in the name of Allah, they are a blot on the history of civilization.

Because all of this leaves a bitter taste, it is easy to pass over the fact that Catholicism and Islam have much in common. Both religions teach that every child is a gift from God with a right to life from the moment of conception – there isn't a single Arab country anywhere in the world where abortion is legal. Muslims also have a positive view of Jesus, believing that He will come again at the end of the world to judge all mankind. A third bond of union, highly significant from an evangelical standpoint, is the esteem that Muslims have for the Blessed Mother. Muslims are frequent visitors at Marian shrines, indeed a whole chapter of the Koran is devoted to Mary, whose virginity is believed by Islam to have been perpetual. I remember recently reading about a newspaper reporter based in the Middle East who, upon entering the bedroom of a Muslim home, was amazed to find a picture of the Virgin Mary as the sole decoration.[5]

When I meet Muslims on the street, I tell them about what happened when Our Lady worked the greatest miracle since the Resurrection at a town named after Muhammad's daughter, Fatima; and, along with the story, I give them a tract to take home with them that describes in detail what no less than 70,000 spectators witnessed (Appendix C).

I would not advise an attempt to pin the charge of terrorism on Islam, as the vast majority of Muslims are non-violent. According to Pope Francis, there's nothing in the Koran, properly interpreted, that calls for murderous *jihad*.[6] Muslims who are devout tend to be friendlier to Christians than those who aren't.[7] In places like Kazakhstan, friendship and marriage between members of the two religions are widely accepted. Indonesia is the world's most populous Muslim nation, and one of its largest organizations, Muhammadya, runs a network of schools that is friendly to Christians. The followers of Jesus are a small minority in Indonesia, but in areas of the country where they are more numerous, Muhammadya sees to it that they are provided with Christian instruction.

Another subject to avoid is women's rights. Few Muslim women of the Middle or Far East are anxious to trade places with their opposite numbers in the West where pornography is rife, abortion is prevalent, and millions of homes are broken. Seventy-five percent of Arab women are full-time mothers who have little desire to raise their children in a society that tolerates same-sex "marriage," regards girls as sex objects, and fails to provide a living wage.[8]

Islam is not generally thought of as a liberalizing force for women. But when Muhammad conquered Arabia in the seventh century, morality was at an all-time low, making life difficult for women, and he introduced a number of reforms that we would call "liberal." Husbands, for example, could no longer pocket the dowries of the wives they divorced. Taking another page from history, the greatest Muslim leaders, including Saladin in the 13th century, held the fair sex in high regard and championed the cause of female education.

In a slender volume entitled *The Great Heresies*, Hilaire Belloc (1870-1953) explains how Islam conquered Christian North Africa. The area was riven by heresy and shot full of corruption – so much so that when the Muslims proved to be able and honest on the whole, they were welcome in many quarters. They introduced a vastly superior justice system for the masses, abolished slavery, and reduced taxation, notwithstanding a discriminatory tax paid by non-Muslims. In short, they were respected for their administrative know-how, along with their vaunted courage, sobriety, and hospitality. Belloc tells of how they got along not only with Christians, but also with Jews who served as mayors of such Islamic strongholds as Cordoba, Granada, and Seville. None of this is surprising – Muslims and Jews were as one in banning graven images, abstaining from pork, and believing in a one-person God.

Why is it important for the Catholic evangelist to know these things? Because the political lay of the land has changed so dramatically in recent years, and there is a tendency nowadays, especially in the industrialized West, to assume that Islam is inherently violent and egregiously anti-woman. Without being minimally aware of another point of view, it is hard to establish common ground, which is the *sine qua non* for religious outreach.

From a strictly theological standpoint, there are two principal obstacles standing in the way of Muslim conversion. The first is an insistence on the part of Islam that someone other than Jesus died on the Cross – an insistence based on a belief that the Father would never have allowed His Son to undergo crucifixion. If you ask Muslims who the "someone" is, they'll say Judas or another surrogate made by God to look and sound miraculously like Jesus. This is absurd from a Christian standpoint. But to exponents of Islam, who view God as arbitrary and capricious, it is perfectly credible. How should one respond?

If Muslims accepted the inerrancy of Christian Scripture, one could point out that Jesus predicted what would happen to Him on Calvary; also that, after rising from the dead, He showed His apostles the nail prints in His hands. But our friends don't believe in Scriptural inerrancy. The genealogies of Jesus given by Matthew and Luke appear contradictory to them, as do the different Gospel accounts of His Resurrection.[9]

THE CHARGE OF TAMPERING

Because encyclopedias of Bible difficulties make quick work of allegations of contradiction, this is not a problem for those willing to do their homework. Yet, we are put to the test when Muslims insist that the Gospels were tampered with, making it appear that Christ claimed divinity when, in fact, He didn't.

The apologist must begin by going to St. Jerome, the great fourth-century Scripture scholar, who claims to have seen an original copy of Matthew's Gospel.[11] If what Jerome says is true, and there is little reason to doubt it, any discrepancies between the original and later, doctored versions would surely have come to light.

But let us say, for the sake of argument, that Jerome was mistaken. We know that all four Gospels record Christ's claim to divinity.[12] We also know that they were written in different places at different times for different audiences. Would there not be too much evidence of falsification in one place or another for the work of a tamperer to escape detection? And once uncovered, would it not have aroused the anger of a faith community that imposed severe penalties for fraud? Can we not assume, too, that the author would have been alerted to any discrepancy between his original manuscript and the so-called "copy" being circulated, if the latter was bogus. There is only one way tampering could have occurred, and that is if someone had gotten hold of all four Gospels, destroyed them, and come out with doctored editions before the originals could circulate. But how likely is this? Hand-written copies of the Gospels (the only ones available before the age of printing) were precious and, as such, would have been jealously guarded.

Another reason to rule out tampering, possibly the most convincing of all, is the existence of Gospel passages that appear to *undermine* the case for Christ's divinity. Why would men bent upon proving Christ's divinity release a text in which the Lord, following His Resurrection, is quoted as saying, "I am ascending to my Father and your Father, and to *my God* and your God?"[13]   And why didn't the alleged culprits delete John

5:19: "The Son [of God] can do nothing of His own accord," along with John 14:28: "the Father is greater than I?"

These and other such passages should be enough, in themselves, to convince anyone with an open mind that the four Gospels are trustworthy. But, for good measure, one might add that three out of four of the Gospel writers, including John, were Jewish, and the Jews of Jesus' time regarded tampering as gravely sinful.[14]

JEWISH TRUTH-TELLING

We know that most of the first Christians were Jewish, and this is significant because Moses forbade the bearing of false witness (Dt. 4:2). We also have Solomon's warning of "Do not add to his [God's] words" (Prov. 30:6). Any priest who falsified or embroidered Sacred Writ was automatically deposed.[15] The Ark of the Covenant, which contained the Ten Commandments, couldn't even be *touched* by unauthorized human hands – in the one recorded instance of such touching, God struck the guilty party dead.

When Josephus combed through a mountain of documentation to write his definitive history of the Jews – tapping Egyptian, Greek, Chaldean (Babylonian), and Tyrian (Lebanese), as well as Jewish sources, many of which have been lost – he found that Hebrew Scripture was every bit as trustworthy as the rabbis maintained.

So highly did the Hebrews value honesty that Sarah's duplicity in denying that she had laughed at the thought of pregnancy in old age became the basis for the exclusion of female testimony in court. The price Jacob paid for his trickery made a lasting impression on God's chosen, as did the leprosy contracted by Elisha's deceitful servant Gehazi. Isaiah condemns duplicity in the harshest of terms, as does Sirach, and we know that such scrupulosity characterized spiritual leaders down to the time of Jesus. According to Rabbi Shammai, a contemporary of Our Lord, one could not even tell a homely bride on the day of her wedding that she was beautiful.

This is why Jesus' description of Nathaniel as a "true Israelite without guile" says as much about first-century Jews as it does about Nathaniel. It is also why Tacitus (c. 55-117 A.D.), the most eminent historian of the period and a man who looked down on the Jews – he viewed them as "singularly prone to lust" – held them superior in one respect: they were "inflexibly honest."[16]

CHRISTIAN TRUTH-TELLING

According to Muslim tradition, it is permissible to twist or distort the truth in order to instill virtue or foster submission to the law. But not so for first century Christians. If the Jews of the period were sticklers for honesty, the Christians, who were mainly of Jewish ancestry, raised the bar even higher.

Pliny the Younger (d. 113) observed, in his letters to the Emperor, that they were bound by oath never to falsify their word or go back on a pledge. The earliest Christian conduct book outside of the Bible, the *Didaché*, goes so far as to forbid equivocation, and early in the second century, Aristedes, alluding to the apostles' emphasis on truth telling, put honesty on a par with compassion as a Christian virtue.

The New Testament is heavy on truth telling. Lying is associated with murder and idolatry.[17] Satan is dubbed "the father of lies" (John 8:44), and Ananias is struck dead mercly for misinforming Peter about his contribution to the common purse. We know that Jesus prayed twice in rapid succession that his followers be "sanctified" in the truth. Did His prayers go unanswered? We also know that He who called Himself "the Way, and the Truth, and the Life" promised that the truth would make us free.

If we look further, we find that Peter condemns deceitfulness many times over; Paul bids us gird our loins with the truth; and James credits truth with giving us birth. As for John, he begins his Gospel by picturing God as "full of truth" and ends it by affirming his own veracity.[18] The word "truth" pops up everywhere, appearing several times within a few lines.[19] It is John who states that all who are "of the truth" will hearken to Jesus, whose *raison d'être* was "to bear witness to the truth." And in his Book of Revelation, he serves notice on anyone who "adds" to Scripture, warning that "God will add to him the plagues" (Rev. 22:18).

Christians have lost much of their reputation for truth telling. But the tradition of the early Church was slow to die. Eusebius (c. 260-339), the first Christian historian of prominence, broke with custom by refusing to put unverifiable words into the mouths of his protagonists, and Augustine observed during the 300s that the slightest deviation from the authorized text on the part of a lector was loudly protested. Add another nine hundred years, and we find Thomas Aquinas insisting on absolute integrity of speech. As late as the 19th century, Victor Hugo presents the lovable Sister Simplice of *Les Miserables* as a woman who never lies. When forced to do so in order to protect her kindly master from arrest by a cruel enemy, she thinks she will faint. Even today, the *Catechism of the Catholic Church* (1994) condemns flattery even when one's goal is to avoid evil.

In the final analysis, it is hard to deny that the Gospels tell us the honest truth about Jesus.

REACHING OUT TO OUR JEWISH BRETHREN

Any dialogue with our Jewish brethren must begin with an expression of respect. Judaism is not only a great religion highly regarded by the Catholic Church. It is the *foundation* for Catholicism. A great saint, John Paul II, referred to the Jewish people as "our beloved brothers in the faith of Abraham, our Patriarch." And so it is. How can one fail to feel a special kinship with those whose Scripture is proclaimed during every Mass as "the word of God?" Or fail to rejoice at the celebration of Hanukah and Passover?

One day, a young man in a black hat and curls came up to me and asked if I was Jewish. "More so, I dare say, than you are," I replied with a twinkle in my eye, "because I'm Catholic. If you search Hebrew Scripture, you'll find many things integral to the Church of Rome – priests, altars, sacrifices, a queen mother, even a high priest who was ordained by God to be the final authority on faith and morals."[20] What began as a friendly chat, ended with an exchange of printed material. I gave him my blessing, and he gave me his – in Hebrew after removing his yarmulke and placing it on my head!

In conversing with your Jewish friends on the street, let them know, as you would anyone else, why we are Christian and Catholic (via the five-point brief for belief spelled out earlier). But don't stop there. Have a tract on hand that lists all of the messianic prophecies. It is clear from the Greek version of Hebrew Scripture (the Septuagint) that Isaiah expected the Messiah to be born of a virgin. Micah names Bethlehem as the place of His birth; Daniel foretells the time of His coming; other prophets anticipate His divinity; still others lay out the exact details of His passion and death. It is all rather remarkable, and I have it from a Jewish university chaplain that none of the alternative interpretations is particularly persuasive (see Appendix D).

THREE PERSONS IN ONE GOD

The main stumbling block for Jews is the Trinity in light of the Old Testament's teaching that God is one.[21] God is indeed one, even for us, but one in three. This is a great mystery. Other than offering proofs for Christ's divinity, pointing out the revelation of the Trinity, and affirming that God can do anything, there is little one can do except to suggest that God gives us a foretaste of the Incarnation in the Old Testament by taking the form of man, much the way angels have done. Abraham entertains three people who are clearly otherworldly, calling one of them "judge of all the world" and "my Lord" (Yahweh in Hebrew).[22] Jacob, after wrestling with a divine personage, says, "I saw God face to face" and names the place of his encounter Peniel, which means "face of God."[23] Some have supposed that Jacob wrestled with an angel, but this is unlikely because every time angels walk the earth in the form of man, they are identified by name.

A third theophany is contained in the Book of Joshua. A man who claims to be the captain of the Jewish army tells Joshua, the worldly captain, to take off his sandals because he is treading on sacred ground, which is what God bids Moses do at the burning bush. Whereupon Joshua falls down and "worships" the man who calls himself captain, something he would never have done for an angel.[24]

COMMON GROUND

During your conversation with a fellow son of Abraham, be sure to highlight the amazing continuity between the Old and New Testaments. We know, for example, that many Jewish priests joined the Church (Acts 6:7), perhaps in recognition of Christianity as the fulfillment of Old Testament prophecy. Ezekiel promised that God's sanctuary would last forever, and Sirach describes the priesthood as an institution that will never pass away.[25]

The linkages between the Old Covenant and the New are too numerous to mention. Catholic churches are open every day, just as the Temple was, and there is daily sacrifice. The costliness of appointments, the splendor of priestly vestments, the grandeur of architectural design – all of this conforms to the specifications laid down by God in the Book of Exodus. The vigil lamp that illuminates Catholic tabernacles is the same as the one that burned twenty-four hours a day in the Temple. Catholic use of holy water and the washing of the priest's hands are based on the Jewish practice of ablution.[26]

On can go further. The ringing of bells at the consecration of the Mass to signal the coming of the Lord echoes the bells that sounded from the garments of the high priest when he made his grand entrance. The miter that belonged to the high priest (Lev. 8:9) is now worn by the bishop. Moses' requirement of weekly assembly is enforced, and the use of incense at Benediction and at a solemn high Mass recalls not only the gift of the Magi and the manner in which Gabriel appeared to Zachary (in a cloud of incense), but also the burning of incense by Moses, Judith, and Jewish priests.

Jesus, the son of a Jewish mother, told his followers to observe and do all that the scribes and Pharisees taught, without following their example.[27] He had not come to abolish the Law, He said, but rather to "fulfill" it, and in line with this, He guaranteed that "not an iota, not a jot" of the Ten Commandments or the teaching of the prophets would pass away until all had been accomplished.[28] Although he introduced much that was new, Our Lord was anything but revolutionary. While He tightened the rules on divorce and remarriage, He was squarely in line with the Book of Malachi, which describes God as hating divorce (Mal. 2:16). His aim was merely to restore marriage to what it had been "from the beginning."[29]

We have seen how, under the New Covenant, celibacy – a privilege hitherto reserved for scribes who were regarded as "married" to their work – was open to all and, in fact, recommended to the apostles.[30] Yet, even here there were precedents, as Roy Varghese has shown. Once the Jewish prophets answered God's call, they appear to have lived as if they were celibate. The priests of the Old Testament abstained from marital relations while on Temple duty, and, of course, the priests of the New are expected to officiate every day of their lives.

Earlier, we mentioned that Our Lord broke with convention when He spoke with a woman whom He didn't know. He also cured on the Sabbath, dispensed with ritual ablution, and downgraded the importance of dietary regulations. But from the day Mary presented Him in the Temple to the day He surrendered in the Garden of Gethsemane, He submitted to the judgment of the high priest. Growing up, He attended services at the local synagogue. Once a year, He accompanied His family on the long journey to Jerusalem to celebrate the Feast of Passover even though this was not required for those who lived far from the Temple.[31] Although He must have shocked His contemporaries by taking a whip to the moneychangers, His aim here, as elsewhere, was strictly conservative: to restore God's sanctuary to its proper function as a "house of prayer."

Christian baptism replaced circumcision as a sign of initiation, but once again, the use of water to signify conversion was not new. As David Goldstein, a 20th century convert from Judaism, observes in his *Letters to Mr. Isaacs*:

> Baptism by immersion preceded the ceremony of circumcision of converts (proselytes of righteousness), who, when they stepped out of the water, were each considered by the Rabbis to be "as if he were a little child just born." Mikwa is the name of the ritual of purification, baptism by immersion in running water, to which high priests, women at childbirth or after menstruation, etc. were obliged to submit (p. 178).

Far from objecting to the Jewish ecclesiastical establishment, Jesus sent His followers to the priests for the certification of cures. His description of Himself as the Good Shepherd was borrowed from Jewish Scripture, as were most of the Beatitudes, along with a fair portion of Mary's *Magnificat* and the *Our Father*. The Christian commandment that one must love one's neighbor as one loves oneself is vintage Old Testament (Lev. 19:18); likewise the obligation to love one's enemy. Exodus and Proverbs stipulate that if one's enemy is hungry, one must give him food, and if his ox or ass goes astray, one must return it to him.[32]

Following the Ascension, Christ's apostles were continually in the Temple, the seat of the Jewish establishment.[33] On the road, they preached in synagogues. Paul continued to support the Jewish nation financially long after his conversion, and upon the completion of his missionary journeys, he registered his Nazirite vow with the Temple authorities.[34] So slow were the early Christians to chart an independent course that it took them twenty years to waive circumcision as a requirement for Gentile conversion, and in order not to appear to be competing openly with the Jewish clergy, they started off by calling their priests "elders." When the Temple fell in 70 A.D., bringing down the Jewish priesthood, these "elders" (or presbyters), who had been equipped ever since the Last Supper to offer Jesus as the Lamb of God in unbloody sacrifice (John 1:29), merely continued to do what they had been doing all along, offering the "clean oblation" prophesied by Malachi.[35]

OBJECTION TO PROSELYTISM

As an aside, it should be added that there are Jews who resent Christian proselytism – so much so that the US Conference of Catholic Bishops (USCCB) published a position paper not long ago declaring them "off limits" for evangelization owing to the so-called "dual covenant" theory. Needless to say, the USCCB paper flew in the face of history and tradition – Peter and his fellow apostles were scourged for taking their message to the streets of Jerusalem, and before the time of Christ, Judaism was itself a missionary religion, seeking converts far and near.[36] In the end, the bishops reversed themselves and deleted all reference to the "dual covenant" from their catechism.[37]

JEWISH EVIDENCE
FOR CHRISTIAN TRUTH TELLING

Some of the best evidence for the reliability of the Gospels comes from Jewish sources. Pinchas Lapide, world-renowned scholar and Israeli diplomat, published one of the most compelling briefs ever written for the Resurrection even though Lapide didn't accept Christ's divinity: *The Resurrection of Jesus* (Munich, 1977; Minnesota, 1983). In addition, there is the evidence of Flavius Josephus (c. 35-95 AD), a general and priest of the lineage of Aaron, as well as one of the greatest historians of his age. Josephus relates things about early Christianity that one would never know from the Gospels, and nothing he says contradicts anything found in the New Testament. On the contrary, he offers evidence for the Resurrection and writes sympathetically about John the Baptist, as well as James, the martyred bishop of Jerusalem.

The Jews we are likely to meet today don't know much about Josephus even though he is honorably mentioned in both the first edition of the Jewish Encyclopedia and the Talmud, the second holiest of all Jewish books next to the Torah.

Josephus died, as he was born, a Jew. And so there can be little question of his objectivity. Skeptics have claimed that Christian propagandists doctored his history. But this is pure speculation, similar in kind to Muslim charges of New Testament tampering. It simply will not hold up under close scrutiny. All the surviving copies of Josephus from various parts of the world in various editions bear the same pro-Christian message. All give the same testimony, the sole exception being a copy in which pro-Christian passages *have been erased!*

The unexpurgated Babylonian version of the Talmud, still another example of a Jewish source that verifies Christian claims, appears to vouch for the fact that Jesus went to Egypt, worked miracles, and was crucified on the eve of Passover.[38] There is even reference to the amnesty granted Barabbas on Good Friday.[39]

According to the Gospel, there was an earthquake that day, causing the veil of the Temple to be torn in two from top to bottom, and again, there is Jewish confirmation. The splitting of the veil is mentioned in the Talmud, and an earthquake may be inferred from the fact that the huge bronze gate of the Temple, a portal so heavy that twenty men were normally required to open it, swung open of its own accord in 30 AD, the likeliest year for the crucifixion.[40]

We learn from the same source that certain miraculous events, which had been occurring on an annual basis in the Temple precincts, ceased taking place in 30 A.D. and were never again reported.[41]

Finally, it is hard to imagine any better evidence for the transformational power of Christ's Passion and Death than two salient facts: Jewish blood sacrifice ended forty years after Jesus offered Himself on Calvary, and Jewish prophecy ended with the start of the Christian era.[42]

The original story circulated by Scribes and Pharisees is that Jesus' body was stolen from the tomb. But this is not something one is likely to hear on the street because it leaves too many questions unanswered. Why would a demoralized group of Christians risk their lives to recover a corpse from a well-guarded tomb? Why, furthermore, would they take the time to remove the burial clothes and fold the face cloth before spiriting their prize away?[43] Even if they had done the unthinkable, how could they have kept it secret? How is one to explain the sudden explosion of apostolic zeal without positing a Resurrection? And finally, why would Christians in great numbers have submitted to gruesome torture and execution for a story they knew to be false?

What you *will* hear on the street is that Catholics didn't do enough to save Jewish lives during World War II. Traceable to *The Deputy*, a German play inspired by Russian Communists, the charge is belied by hard, cold facts. Catholics are estimated to have saved something on the order of 800,000 Jews. Many were hidden in monasteries and convents, as well as in the Vatican itself. Scores of articles and books have been written in defense of the Church. But when this question crops up on the street, I recommend Rabbi David Dalin's *The Pius War* (2004).

While Catholic leaders may not have done all in their power to save the victims of Nazi genocide, they did more than all other organizations put together. Why, if Catholics were remiss, did Israel Zolli, the chief rabbi of Rome, convert to Catholicism after the war with nothing to gain and everything to lose? No one can deny that many Catholics risked their livelihoods, and even their lives, to save members of a group that had never been known for its cordiality toward the Church. What would have happened, one wonders, if the shoe had been on the other foot? If Jews, in other words, had been called upon to shelter Catholics, as was the case during Rome's imperial persecution.

CHAPTER 7

CONVERSING WITH PROTESTANTS, JEHOVAH'S WITNESSES, AND MORMONS

When we speak of "separated brethren" in this chapter, the term will not be used in reference to high church Protestants or members of Eastern Orthodox churches because we've already argued the case for marital indissolubility and papal teaching authority – the principal points differentiating our church from theirs. Instead, we will be examining practical ways of engaging low-church Protestants, who are actually closer to us on issues of sexual morality and therefore more open, in many cases, to conversion. Truth be told, they are more "Catholic" than we are when it comes to attitudes toward legalization of abortion, same-sex "marriage," prayer in the classroom, prayer at graduation ceremonies, and the use of public school facilities for religious purposes after hours. Although statistics indicate that they are less likely than we are to regard weekly church attendance as imperative, they are more likely to *act* as if they did. They are more apt to tithe, and lastly, in the area of Bible study, homiletics, and evangelization, they are miles ahead of us.[1]

In any encounter, after the usual expression of respect and esteem, along with a review of common ground, we must spell out the reason why we are Catholic – point #4 of the brief for belief mentioned earlier. Our listeners will respond by telling us where they think Catholics have gone wrong, and we reply in kind. But before discussing strategies of engagement, we need to correct a number of mistaken impressions that could stand in the way of winning the hearts of Protestants. We may think, for instance, that they favor a literal interpretation of Scripture. They may think so, too. But is this really true? Who takes Jesus' words on the Eucharist literally (John 6)? Who is the literalist when it comes to attendance at weekly assembly, as required by Leviticus 23:2-3 and Hebrews 10:25? Jesus recommended celibacy and poverty for church leaders, and again, who takes such preferences at face value?

Another example of strict adherence to the text on the part, not of Protestants, but rather of the Catholic Church, is its insistence on the indissolubility of marriage. Paul is unequivocal in his condemnation of remarriage after divorce, as is Jesus in the Gospels of Mark and Luke. Matthew's account is cited by many of our separated brethren as an exception. But where is the evidence? The Greek word *porneia* in the nineteenth chapter of Matthew (verse 9) means fornication, and this is the way most Catholic scholars over the years have translated it. Protestant reformers, on the other hand, in their refusal to take *porneia* literally, stretched it to mean adultery. If Jesus wanted to make an exception for adultery, why didn't He say so? There was an Aramaic word for adultery. Why didn't He use it? Why is Matthew's so-called "escape" clause not found in Mark, Luke, or Paul? John doesn't even address the question of remarriage after divorce, suggesting that by the time he wrote the Fourth Gospel, Christian teaching was clear. Why, finally, if *porneia* meant adultery is there is no record of divorce in the early Church?

We shall pass over the fact that when Protestants opted for a loose translation of *porneia*, they found themselves on a slippery slope. Over the years, as morals collapsed, they wound up substituting even looser terms such as "immorality" and "unchastity" (for "adultery") until they accepted spousal discontent of almost any kind as a justification for divorce and remarriage.

A second error commonly made in sizing up Protestants – Fundamentalists and Evangelicals in particular – is to assume that those who take the Genesis account of creation at face value do so *because they are literalists*. They do it for the same reason Catholics take John 6 literally: they think it means what it says. Most of today's Catholic intellectuals subscribe to the theory of evolution. But the Church, as a church, has never taken a stand on this issue. And why should it? As previously mentioned, evolution is simply a theory yet to be proven. Why wave a red flag in the face of would-be converts? Those who have the spine to buck conventional wisdom on the origin of human life might embrace other unconventional ideas – such as transubstantiation and papal infallibility.

Another factor militating against outreach to low church Protestantism is pejorative use of the word "Fundamentalist." Originally, the term referred to Protestants who, in resisting biblical skepticism, committed themselves to six "fundamental" dogmas: biblical inerrancy, the Virgin birth, Christ's divinity, the substitutionary atonement of His death, His Resurrection, and His literal return at the Second Coming. Needless to say, every one of these positions coincides with what the Catholic Church has taught for two thousand years.

While we are at it, "Puritanical" is yet another word that lends itself to caricature. The New Englanders of the 17th century loved games, they had large families, and yes, they banned theater, dance, gambling, and alcoholic beverages without a sound basis in the Bible. But there is nothing to indicate that they were particularly ascetical. And what if they were? Who are we, as Catholics, to turn up our noses at folks who may have practiced bodily mortification? Our saints went in for it on a scale unimaginable to most members of the Massachusetts Bay Colony.

WHY THE BIBLE ALONE?

To return, though, to the conversation we are likely to have on the street with low church Protestants, we need to ask them why they subscribe to Luther's doctrine of *sola Scriptura* (Scripture alone as a source of truth) because it has no basis in Scripture. The verse most often cited in its defense – 2 Tim. 3:16 – describes Scripture as useful in its entirety "that the man of God may be fully competent and equipped for every good work." But usefulness and sufficiency are two different things. A fisherman may say to a friend, "I'm going away on vacation. Feel free to use my tackle box until I get back, because it contains lures that you lack. This way, you'll be fully equipped." Left unsaid is the fact that the friend will need a rod and a boat. All of Scripture is useful, but this does not make it sufficient because the Word does not interpret itself. As Shakespeare's Bassanio observes, "In religion what damned error but some sober brow will bless it, and approve it with a text."[2]

Within ten years of the launching of the Reformation, there were half a dozen interpretations of the meaning of the Eucharist, which is why Scripture provides for a divinely ordained interpreter.[3] There are scores of thousands of Protestant sects today, all differing on dogma, yet claiming the inspiration of the Holy Spirit. How can this be? Does the Holy Spirit have a forked tongue? Is the Third Person of the Blessed Trinity a liar? *Sola Scriptura* not only leads to the kind of division and sectarianism condemned by Peter and Paul. It is also grist for the mill of our enemies.

THE CHURCH AND THE BIBLE

Many non-Catholics are under the impression that the Church added books to the sacred canon during the Middle Ages when, in fact, it was the "reformers" who deleted them. We are speaking of the so-called deuterocanonical or apocryphal books, which are objectionable from a Protestant standpoint because, in addition to supporting prayer for the dead and the doctrine of free will, they describe the priesthood as eternal.

The case for Catholic inclusion of the books is uncomplicated. All seven of the books in question were included in the Septuagint, the Greek version of Hebrew Scripture, and we know that this was the version favored by Jesus and His apostles, because, as pointed out earlier, eighty percent of the Old Testament quotations found in the New Testament are taken from it. Secondly, the deuterocanonical books were accepted as the word of God by just about all believers from the dawn of Christian history down to the time of Martin Luther. How much sense does it make to assume that the "Advocate" sent by Jesus to lead His Church to the fullness of truth was off duty for fifteen hundred years? Thirdly, the deleted books are magnificent, chronicling, as they do, the heroism of Judith and the Maccabees. The Book of Wisdom is sublime, and Sirach, which was the conduct book of the early Church, is superior, in many ways, to Proverbs.

As far as translations are concerned, I use the King James Version (KJV) on the street because it is the only one many of my Protestant friends will listen to. I can make all my points from it, including the fact that the original KJV contained the deuterocanonicals! And in some respects, I find it superior to many Catholic editions. Among other things, it translates *porneia* as fornication.[4]

There are critics who claim that medieval priests tried to keep folks from the Bible by chaining it inside churches and burning certain versions. Bibles were indeed chained, but only to ensure their availability. Before the invention of the printing press (c. 1430), they were hand-copied, a process that made the cost of ownership prohibitively high – the equivalent of a year's wages. Was the Church that brought out the first vernacular editions, beginning with St. Jerome's Vulgate, trying to keep Scripture from the people?

If books were burned, it was to shield the faithful from heretical translation and annotation. Much of it occurred in France during the twelfth and thirteenth centuries when Albigensians, who controlled large swathes of territory in the southeast part of the country, had put out versions of the Word that undermined the institution of marriage. One might add, too, that book burning was not a particularly Catholic thing. Henry VIII did it in post-Reformation England.

WHY FAITH ALONE?

Next to *sola Scriptura*, there is nothing more characteristically Protestant than the doctrine of *sola fide* (salvation by faith alone). No matter that the phrase "faith alone" occurs only once in the Bible, and when it does (in the Letter of James), it vindicates the Catholic position: "By works a man is justified and not by faith alone ... faith without works is dead."[5] Luther wanted to strike the Letter of James from the canon and would probably have done so had it not been for the veto power of fellow reformers. Instead, he brought out his own version of the Bible and added the word "alone" to the twentieth-eighth verse of the third chapter of Paul's Letter to the Romans, thereby changing its meaning.

Whether you are on the street or in private conversation, it is important to make clear that Catholics don't expect to "earn" a place in heaven by doing good. Many Protestants, on hearing this, will be taken aback because it is not what they were taught to believe about us. The Church is well aware of Romans 11:6 and other passages that rule out the possibility of "bartering" with God. Nothing on the part of finite creatures can atone for offenses against a Being who is infinite. Hence the need for divine intervention. But although we, as Catholics, don't see ourselves as "earning" salvation, we believe we can and must "deserve" it by cooperating with God's grace. Jesus Himself says, "If thou wilt enter into life, keep the commandments."[6] Peter is just as clear, God "judgeth according to every man's work."[7]

If your friend counters with John 6:47, "He that believeth ... has everlasting life," ask him why Scripture promises a "reward" for works. According to James, the man who "endures temptation" is blessed, for "when he has been tried, he will receive the crown of life."[8] Paul prophesies that Alexander, who opposed him in Ephesus, will be repaid "according to his works."[9] Jesus is even more specific. Anyone who suffers persecution, gives anonymously, fasts in secret, welcomes a prophet, or uses his God-given talent is on his rewards list. The same holds true for those who love their enemies, lend without hope of reward, or entertain guests who cannot reciprocate.[10]

Another Protestant misconception is the belief that Catholics live in constant fear of damnation. All one needs to do in this instance is explain that while we don't regard salvation as a given, we have more than enough assurance to be filled with joy. Venial sin will not keep us out of heaven, and those who are serious about the Faith will rarely, if ever, commit any other kind of sin. But even if they do, God will not send them to hell provided they are resolved (a) to go to confession, and (b) to amend their lives. For Catholics who are marooned on a desert island with no priest to hear their confession, the mere fact of contrition, combined with a firm resolve to sin no more, will suffice. In sum, the conditional certainty of the Catholic is more reassuring than the unconditional certainty of Protestants who lack a firm basis in Scripture for their belief. More on this in a moment.

Those who believe in the sufficiency of faith or *sola fide* may be counting on a faith that is strong enough to ensure good works – "once saved, always saved." But how can this be? Common sense, which suggests that faith can be lost, is confirmed by Jesus, who warns that those who receive the word with joy can fall away when faced with trouble or persecution.[11] Scripture tells us, in addition, that those who *persevere* to the end will be saved.[12] Why *persevere*? Why do we read in Peter's Second Letter, "Beware lest ye … fall from your own steadfastness?"[13] Why does John write, "Look to yourselves that you do not lose what you have worked for?"[14]

No one is more quotable from a Protestant standpoint than Paul. But what does the man from Tarsus have to say?

> Work out your own salvation with fear and trembling
> ... I do not consider that I have laid hold of it already
> ... I press on toward the goal to the prize of God's
> heavenly call ... I chastise my body and bring it into
> subjection lest perhaps, after preaching to others,
> I myself should be rejected ... Let him who thinks
> he stands take heed lest he fall ... I fear lest ... your
> minds be corrupted and you fall from a single-hearted
> devotion to Christ. [15]

Those who subscribe to the doctrine of *sola fide* will quote Paul's Letter to the Romans: "By grace are ye saved ... not of yourselves: it is the gift of God; not of works, lest any man should boast" and "a man is justified by faith without the deeds of the law."[16] Fair and square. But we can quote from the same letter: God "will render to every man according to his works."[17] We also have at our disposal Paul's list of sins that shut a man out of heaven.[18] Faithlessness is not one of them.

Proof texting over an extended period of time gets tiresome. Don't hesitate, therefore, to break if off by handing out a summary of all the things Jesus Himself said that bear on the issue under discussion:

> By their fruits you will know them... . Every tree that
> does not bear good fruit is cut down and thrown into
> the fire ... . Not everyone who says to me, 'Lord, Lord'
> shall enter the kingdom of heaven; but he who does
> the will of my Father in heaven ... Anyone who hears
> my words and does not act upon them shall be likened
> to a foolish man who built his house on sand ... [he]
> was utterly ruined... . [God, at the Last Judgment]
> will render to everyone according to his conduct... .
> If thou wilt enter into life, keep the commandments
> ... [The unprofitable servant will be] cast forth into
> the darkness ... where there will be the weeping and
> the gnashing of teeth... . [God will say to those who
> sinned grievously] depart from me, accursed ones,

into the everlasting fire which was prepared for the
devil and his angels. For I was hungry and you did
not give me to eat; I was thirsty and you did not give
me to drink; I was a stranger and you did not take me
in … Blessed are they who hear the word of God and
keep it… . He who has my commandments and keeps
them, he is it who loves me … if anyone loves me, he
will keep my word … You are my friends if you do the
things I command you. [19]

As a street evangelist, you may feel, at this point, that you've
exhausted all the evidence and reached an impasse, but in fact
you've arrived at the most important stage of the discussion – the
one where you ask your Protestant friend if he thinks the entire
Bible is the word of God. If his answer is "yes," as will almost
always be the case, ask him if God can contradict Himself. This
he will surely deny, paving the way for you to draw a couple of
conclusions: (1) one cannot interpret Scripture in such a way as
to render it internally inconsistent, and (2) those who have the
least amount of difficulty reconciling apparent contradiction
possess the fullness of the truth.

Having come this far, you occupy high ground because
your intellectual framework as a Catholic is broad enough to
accommodate Scripture in its entirety. Passages interpreted by
Protestants as negating the need for works can be identified as
references not to the Ten Commandments, but rather to practices such as circumcision that pertain to ritual and hygiene. The
key to reconciling apparently contradictory passages lies in the
verses that precede or follow the "faith" passages. John 3:16, for
example, seems to support *sola fide*, but not when read in conjunction with John 3:36 in the RSV translation, which is true to
the Greek and which mandates obedience to God's commands.
Similarly, in the case of Ephesians 2:8-9, which seems dismissive

of the need for works; its meaning becomes clear the moment it is placed alongside Ephesians 2:11. Or take Romans 1:17, a "faith" passage that must be read in conjunction with Romans 2:6. As the saying goes, "proof text without context is pretext." Verses such as Romans 3:29-30; 9:30; and 10:12 are sure to be misunderstood by anyone who fails to take all relevant passages into account.

Some time ago, I wrote many pages, single-spaced, in response to questions from a Protestant evangelist. He mailed me a ton of anti-Catholic literature – so much that I began to suspect he was in someone's pay. No sooner did I reply to one set of questions than I received another. And what really irked me was the fact that he never responded to my replies. Was he simply tossing my work into the circular file? The game was not worth the candle, and so I broke off the correspondence – gently, but firmly:

> Perhaps we should give our dialogue a breather. I'll pray for you. Please pray for me. The third person of the Blessed Trinity doesn't generally rain down all His wisdom at once. So I'll keep an open mind, trusting that you'll do the same.

> Please give some thought to my responses and take a look at the books I recommended. If your conscience tells you to remain where you are after you've done your best to inform it, then you have no other choice. All I ask is that you take care not to misrepresent the Catholic faith, as this would be a violation of the eighth Commandment.

In retrospect, I realize that, after answering a few of my friend's questions I should have raised questions of my own concerning the failure of Protestantism to conform to biblical specifications. Why should Catholics have to do all the explaining?

Another incident illustrative of the practical side of evangelization occurred at Grand Central Terminal. A couple of Protestant pastors stopped by, and we had a lively discussion about the Faith. It was late in the afternoon, and after about forty-five minutes of spirited give-and-take, I told them I had to head home for dinner. Much to my surprise, they suggested that we continue the exchange at a local coffee shop, and I was happy to agree. Normally, I would have been concerned about holding my own in a two-against-one type of format. But I knew of a device that would ensure equal talking time: my wife's kitchen timer. It served the purpose admirably. Seven hours of earnest back-and-forth discussion spread over several days at a local Starbucks turned out to be highly rewarding. Every five minutes, the alarm would go off, signaling that it was time for the speaking side to yield. In this way, we were never plagued with either of the two elements most likely to impede communication: chaos and discourtesy.

One final story from the street. Last year, a Protestant evangelist handed me a Chick tract characterizing veneration of Mary as blasphemous "worship" and bending other aspects of Catholic devotion way out of shape. I'd seen Chick publications before. Typically, they set up a straw man and knock it down. So I sent the man a seven-page, single-spaced refutation and offered to join him for a cup of coffee. When he declined the invitation, I wasn't surprised. Neither was I surprised to see him back on the street a few days later, handing out the same tracts. "Still at it?" I asked. "I wouldn't want to be in your shoes on Judgment Day. You have every right to disagree with what the Church's teaches, but God will hold you responsible for deliberate falsification. Scripture has it that 'Thou shalt not bear false witness against thy neighbor.' " He didn't say a word, and this was the last I saw of him.

ENGAGING JEHOVAH'S WITNESSES

Jehovah's Witnesses, a familiar sight on the street, are neatly dressed and cheerful. Anyone who gives evidence of believing in a power higher than himself or herself lifts my spirits. And so I commend them for their zeal and suggest that in the battle against secular materialism, people of faith must pull together. Needless to say, this doesn't always elicit a positive response. But I say it anyway, knowing that a spirit of generosity can't do any harm. Sometimes it is the only way to pry open hearts and minds that would otherwise remain closed.

After exchanging pleasantries, I begin asking questions about the Witnesses to avoid being on the receiving end of a lengthy, well-rehearsed speech that I've heard many times over. "If you can give me a satisfactory answer to a couple of questions regarding your faith," I tell them with a smile, "I'll consider becoming a Jehovah's Witness. If not, you'll have to give some thought to becoming Catholic!" Normally, they are more than happy to lend me their ear, and here are the questions that I ask.

QUESTION #1

"Since you believe it's wrong to kill, even in self-defense, you won't serve as a police officer or soldier. But suppose everyone felt this way. How long would we be safe from terrorists? How long would the United States remain free and independent as a nation?" One of the drawing cards of the Witnesses is their exemption from the draft on the basis of conscientious objection. It's hard to understand, however, how anyone who is patriotic can be attracted to an organization that prohibits the use of arms, even in self defense – an organization, moreover, that tells its members they may not vote, run for political office, salute the flag, or recite the Pledge of Allegiance.

I've yet to receive a satisfactory answer to my first question. But I don't leave it there. "Show me pacifism in the Bible," I continue. "In the Old Testament, God orders the Israelites into battle, and in the New Testament, John the Baptist tells soldiers to be content with their pay.[20] Jesus instructs His followers to 'Render to Caesar the things that are Caesar's' and praises a Roman centurion for having faith greater than anything seen in Israel."[21] "Where," I ask, "is pacifism at the Last Supper, when Our Lord says to His apostles, 'Let him who has no sword sell his tunic and buy one'? They reply, 'Lord, behold, here are two swords,' and His response is 'Enough.'"[22]

It has been suggested that the swords mentioned at the Last Supper were solely for protection against animals. But why swords? Why not the all-purpose staff mentioned by Luke?[23] The apostolic band spent years traversing the countryside where wolves and lions were more of a threat than they could ever have been in Jerusalem. Why would Jesus wait until the Last Supper to bring up the subject of physical safety?

The Witnesses (JWs) are fond of citing Christ's counsel to turn the other cheek. I tell them that, as Catholics, we believe that what Our Lord had in mind was personal reaction to insult or injury, rather than the response of a nation to foreign invasion. I then ask if they remember the time Jewish leaders were about to arrest Jesus in the Garden of Gethsemane. His apostles asked him, "Shall we strike with the sword?" And before He could reply, Peter drew his weapon and cut off the ear of the servant of the High Priest.[24] "Would the apostles talk or act this way," I ask, "if they'd been pacifists?" "Would they carry weapons, much less use them?" Your friend may remind you of Our Lord's order to Peter to put away his sword. But the wording of the order – "bear with them *thus far*" – implies that Christians will fight in the future.[25]

Another JW favorite is Jesus' insistence that those who live by the sword will die by it.[26] Again, there is a Catholic answer. Christ was not about to deny lawfully constituted authorities the right to arrest Him. He was merely observing that those who draw the sword *against the law* wind up dying by it. He was also anxious to accomplish the purpose for which He had been born: "Shall I not drink the cup that the Father has given me?"[27]

If your JW friends point out that the early Christians refused service in Rome's armies, admit it. This is history. But it had nothing to do with pacifism. Soldiers were required to swear allegiance to the emperor as God, something no serious follower of Jesus would do. Peter and Paul could no more recognize Caesar as the King of Kings than Thomas More could recognize Henry VIII as head of the English church.

QUESTION #2

Why is it that certain passages in the JW *New World Bible* (NWB) are untrue to the original Greek? In Greek, John 1:1 reads, "the Word [i.e. Jesus] was God." But the NWB changes "God" to "a God." This squares with the JW denial of Christ's divinity, but there is no article in the Greek. Again, when Jesus raised bread at the Last Supper, He said, "This is my body." But the Witnesses have Him saying, "This *means* my body." The switch enables them to deny Eucharistic transubstantiation, but it is untenable. Or take Matthew 19 wherein Jesus describes hell as "everlasting fire." Once more, the New World Bible alters the text – this time to read "everlasting *cutting off,*" lending credence to the JW rejection of eternal hellfire.

What more can one say? Tampering with Sacred Scripture is sacrilegious. Among the members of the JW commission who translated the original Greek into English, only one knew Greek, and his training was in classical, rather than New Testament Greek. Which raises the additional question of competence since the classical Greek of Plato and Herodotus differs from that of Luke much the way Chaucer's Old English differs from the language of Dickens.

If you succeed in bringing your friend this far, you will have done well because JW volunteers are relieved of their duty at frequent intervals. And don't expect a satisfactory answer to your questions, even when you are assured that a supervisor will get back to you. Chances are, you will be offered some literature, possibly the latest edition of the JW *Watchtower* magazine. Accept it provided your friend agrees to take a copy of Appendix B. Many Witnesses are ex-Catholics who never studied the Faith, and what they need, more than anything else, is evidence that the religion into which they were born makes sense. For your part, if the material they give you raises questions you can't answer after consulting apologetics books of the kind listed in Appendix F, go to a knowledgeable priest or layman.

For the rest of my questions for Jehovah's Witnesses, along with a list of false predictions they have made regarding the end of the world, see Appendix B. The reason they are there, rather than here in the heart of chapter 7, is that I have never gotten beyond questions 1 and 2 with anyone on the street. At the end of a cordial conversation, I simply offer my friends a photocopy of Appendix B, along with my contact information.

MEETING MORMONS

The Church of Jesus Christ of Latter-day Saints, like the Jehovah's Witnesses, is growing by leaps and bounds. People thrive on challenge, and Mormons are expected to devote two years of their life to missionary work. The women are starting to assume this duty, along with the men. Another drawing card of the CJCLS is a welfare system based on mandatory tithing that ensures the well being of all who suffer from infirmity or old age.

Mormons believe that a Jew named Levi brought a group of fellow Jews to the New World around 600 B.C. – the so-called lost tribes of Israel. According to the *Book of Mormon*, Levi had two sons, Nephi, who was good, and Laman, who was evil. In 421 A.D., the Lamanites massacred the Nephites, and only one of the latter survived – Moroni, son of Mormon. Nephi is said to have brought with him to the western hemisphere ancient records of the Jews, which Mormon handed over to Moroni for safe-keeping, along with records of the Nephites since 600 B.C. and additional "revelations" which were inscribed on gold plates which Moroni buried in Palmyra, New York, east of Rochester. Joseph Smith found these plates, as the story goes, and translated them with the help of miraculous stones called the Urim and Thummim, after which the plates mysteriously disappeared.

Smith won many converts, especially in western New York, along with a host of enemies, causing him to move to Ohio, then to Missouri, and finally to Illinois where he was murdered in 1844. His successor, Brigham Young, led an exodus of Mormons to present-day Salt Lake City, and it was under Young's leadership that Mormonism prospered.

MORMON BELIEFS

1. They "accept" the Bible but claim it was superseded by (a) the *Book of Mormon*, (b) "revelations" given to their founder, Joseph Smith, in the late 1820s; and (c) ongoing revelation given to Smith's successors down to the present day.
2. They believe in Jesus' atonement for sin and His Resurrection from the dead, along with heaven and the Last Judgment. Hell exists, but it is not "everlasting."
3. They do not believe in the Eucharist (Christ's Real Presence), nor do they define marriage as a union between one man and one woman. On the contrary, Joseph Smith received a "revelation" that anyone who does not accept the principle of polygamy, multiple wives, is eternally damned. When Smith was murdered in 1844, he left twenty-seven widows.
4. Mormons believe further that we can all be gods like Jesus and that Mary had carnal relations with God to conceive the Christ child.
5. They claim to be Christians, though the Catholic Church does not recognize them as such or accept their baptism.
6. They are forbidden to smoke, gamble, or drink anything containing alcohol or caffeine.
7. They view the husband as head of the family, and the women wear veils to religious services.

8. They allow divorce, but not fornication or same-sex "marriage." Utah, the Mormon capital of the world, has had one of the nation's highest rates of divorce.

9. Abortion is permissible in cases of rape, incest, or danger to the life of the mother.

PROBLEMS WITH MORMONISM

1. Neither archaeology nor DNA research supports the Mormon claim that the Jews settled in the New World around 600 B.C., and there is no apparent connection between Jews and Native American Indians.

2. There are questions about the golden plates. Three of the witnesses who claimed to have seen them defected from Mormonism, and in a sworn affidavit, the plates were identified as "gotten up" by a blacksmith and "cut out of some pieces of copper."

3. According to sixty-two persons who knew the Smith family, Joseph was a man of loose character and vicious habits, and if the historical record is any indication, this would appear to be true. A scholar named Anthon identified the characters on the plates as Egyptian, Chaldaic, Assyriac, and Arabian. But when Anthon was questioned about this, he denied it. In the second place, worthless notes were issued from a bank Smith established. Thirdly, Smith claimed to have Egyptian papyri that told the story of Abraham. But the papyri wound up in New York's Metropolitan Museum of Art, and when a Mormon Egyptologist translated them, they turned out to be nothing but a funeral text without any reference to Abraham.

In the end, the disillusioned Egyptologist left the Mormon faith.

4. The children of a Rev. Solomon Spalding, a Congregationalist minister who died in 1816, claimed that the *Book of Mormon* (1830) was plagiarized from their father's novel, *Manuscript Found*, which he had circulated privately. When they sued, the case was dismissed because they could not produce the original copy of the novel – it disappeared mysteriously from a print shop in Pittsburgh. But in 1976, three Mormon researchers discovered samples of Spalding's handwriting that were indisputably authentic in the Oberlin College Library. Not long after, while doing research in a Mormon church library, they discovered long passages from the *Book of Mormon* in the exact same handwriting. Two handwriting experts agreed that the handwriting in both cases was unquestionably Spalding's. The Mormons disputed the finding, but their credibility suffered when they refused to allow anyone to examine the relevant document in their library. All three of the researchers who discovered the evidence left the Mormon faith.

5. When the U. S. government refused to allow Utah to apply for admittance to the Union without a ban on polygamy, the Mormons accepted the ban. But they still regard polygamy as ideal and believe it will prevail in heaven.

6. For many years, blacks were excluded from leadership positions in the Mormon church on the assumption that dark skin was God's punishment for sin and a curse. This changed with the advent of the civil rights movement.

7. Mormons believe in many gods despite the Bible's oft-repeated insistence that there is **only one God** (e.g., Isaiah 44:6; 45:5-6).

8. They believe that their Scriptures correct the New Testament even though the Book of Jude (verse 3) states clearly that the Faith was "once for all delivered to the saints."

9. The author of the *Book of Mormon*, Nephi, is supposed to have written his book during the period 600-500 B.C., but parts of it, in English translation, are practically a carbon copy of entire chapters of the King James Bible, which was not published until the 17th century.[28] Why did God choose 17th century King James English to dictate to a 19th century seer?

10. Joseph Smith, the founder of Mormonism, claimed he could translate Egyptian hieroglyphics into English, but when he translated the hieroglyphic identification inscriptions on five figures in an Egyptian painting, he got them all wrong.[29]

11. Smith and his family were treasure hunters, and on one occasion when Smith claimed to have a special seer stone, he was arrested and found guilty of a sham.[30]

12. Among the witnesses to the golden plates from which Smith claimed to have translated the *Book of Mormon*, one changed his faith thirteen times and claimed to have visited the moon. Another was excommunicated for accusing Smith of adultery, and a third was advised to leave the Mormon Church. Smith accused the latter two of being part of a "gang of counterfeiters, thieves, liars, and blacklegs."[31]

13. Mormon leaders have admitted that Smith married some-
    where between thirty and forty wives, some of whom were
    already joined in matrimony to other men, and one of
    whom was a girl of fourteen.[32]

CONCLUSION

The last several chapters have had a strong cutting edge, and rightly so. Apologetics is, by nature, combative. At the same time, I wouldn't want to put the finishing touches on a book dealing with evangelization without, once again, highlighting the need to reach out to non-Catholics with gentleness and respect – Peter's words.[1] One day, while I was on the street, a Jewish lady stopped by to say, "I'm on my way to the synagogue, but I want you to know how much I respect you. Faith is important!" This lady is a model for all of us.

Earlier, we noted that Mother Angelica, America's greatest televangelist, had a great many non-Catholic friends. She loved them for their strengths, and they respected her as a nun. Beyond this, they not only urged her to lead a Lenten Bible study, but also invited her onto their TV shows and helped her build her own sets. Most of the original employees at EWTN were Baptists!

Bishop Sheen, another prime example of evangelical Catholicism, shared Angelica's genius for uniting the Catholic and non-Catholic world. He urged his fellow Catholics to use a Bible commentary by Presbyterian William Barclay, gave retreats for Protestant ministers, and had positive things to say about Muslims. Offers to appear on non-Catholic TV stations and invitations to teach at prestigious secular universities such as Columbia and Oxford followed naturally.

We may not come even with Mother Angelica or Bishop Sheen. But we can walk as they walked. If evangelical Protestants

are good at Bible study, we can say so. If they are exemplary
public witnesses, we can commend them. As long as we don't
shrink from discussing our differences, there is nothing wrong
with encouraging folks who care deeply about what matters
most. Billy Graham produced a magnificent volume on the
problem of pain, *Hope for the Troubled Heart*, and since it contains nothing objectionable from a Catholic standpoint, we are
free to recommend it. Leo Strobel, another Protestant scholar,
has given us what may be the best defense ever written on the
subject of Gospel reliability: *The Case for Christ*. Strobel, like
Graham, deserves our praise.

At a time when religion is under assault across the board,
there is greater need than ever for believers of every kind to unite.
As Benjamin Franklin told embattled fellow patriots during the
Revolution, "If we do not hang together, we will most assur-
edly hang separately!" According to the California Department
of Education, the worst problems faced by school superinten-
dents in 1940 were talking out of turn, chewing gum, making
noise, running in halls, cutting in line, dress code infractions,
and littering. By 1980, the list, in order of importance, con-
sisted of: pregnancy, drug abuse, alcohol abuse, suicide, rape,
robbery, and assault. We have entered a new age of barbarism.
A million infants are slaughtered in their mother's wombs
every year, something unprecedented in human history. An Ivy
League university has hired a professor who defends infanticide.
Cohabitation and sodomy have found widespread acceptance –
when I was a boy, the name for such practices was "mortal sin"!

George Washington observed that, "reason and experience
both forbid us to expect that national morality can prevail in
the exclusion of religious principle." The question, however, is
what kind of religious principle? Catholicism is the only faith

that has shown itself capable of standing firm against the prevailing winds of radical feminism and sexual license, the only one that remains unwavering in opposition to abortion, contraception, divorce, euthanasia, and sodomy. Not without reason did President George W. Bush call it "a rock in a raging sea."

There is one important caveat, however, which brings us full circle to the state of the Church in America. If the "rock in a raging sea" is to stand firm, if our Church is to do what is needed to put America back on track, it can no longer turn its back on evangelization. For many years, it was customary for American Catholics to regard religious outreach as a "Protestant thing," and this is hardly surprising. During the colonial period, when English sovereigns governed us, the mere harboring of a priest was a capital offense. Victory in the War for Independence hinged on the military operations of Catholic Spain, as well as Catholic France, and so "papists" were permitted to practice their faith openly after 1783. Eventually, they were given the vote. But throughout the early national period, residual hatred and distrust precluded any serious venture of an evangelical nature.

For the next hundred years or more, the American Church was engrossed in the building of schools, hospitals, and orphanages. Then, with the end of World War II, came a third phase. Catholics took their place on university campuses. Private clubs began opening their doors. John F. Kennedy became the first of his faith to be elected president.

The downside of it is that Kennedy prevailed by promising never to allow the tenets of his faith to color his views as a public servant. Perhaps he knew that the average layman, along with the average priest, wanted nothing more than to fit in and be accepted. He was right. And what they wanted is what they got. They fit in so well that there's scarcely any difference today between Catholic and Protestant rates of contraception, abortion, and divorce. Called by Rome to go out to others, Catholics erected a bubble around themselves, closed the windows, and shut the doors.

The only question is how long this state of affairs is going to continue before those who receive the oil of Confirmation put on the armor of God and take up Paul's "sword of the spirit." The future, not only of the Church in America, but also of Western civilization, hangs in the balance. When the United States entered World War I, billboards urging young men to enlist in the army showed a huge picture of Uncle Sam pointing his finger with the caption, "Uncle Sam Wants **You!**" Currently, we are at war as never before with the forces of secular materialism, and the man who "wants **you**" is the Holy Father.

Pope Francis, quoted in the introductory pages of this volume, granted an interview to the editor of a Jesuit magazine in Italy, in which he said that, "we need to proclaim the Gospel on every street corner."[2] In like vein, he told fellow cardinals that "when the Church does not come out of itself to evangelize, it … gets sick," it succumbs to "spiritual worldliness … living in itself, of itself, and for itself." None of this was news to Argentinians because they had already heard him say, as Cardinal Bergoglio, that the "mission" of the Church is "to announce the Gospel … a church that limits itself to administering parish work, that lives enclosed within a community, experiences what someone in prison does: physical and mental atrophy."[3]

A medieval saint by the name of Raymond Nonnatus was captured by Muslims and tortured for having the courage to preach. His lips were pierced and padlocked so that he couldn't utter a word except during mealtime. Today, in America, our lips are unlocked. We have more freedom to spread the Gospel than Nonnatus could ever have imagined! And what are we doing?

It is easy to become discouraged at a time when we have sunk to an all-time low morally. But as Warren Carroll points out in his magisterial *History of Christendom*, the Church has survived moral crises in the past every bit as serious as those we are seeing today. The Old Testament, arguably the best behavioral history of mankind ever written, chronicles cycle after cycle of moral collapse on the part of a people who had the truth, followed by chastisement and ... rebirth!

We are people of hope, not despair, and now, as never before, there are signs of what John Paul II called "a new springtime" of faith. Let us, therefore, lift up our hearts. Whether we are confined to a hospice or serving as head of a major corporation – whatever our situation – we have an important part to play in the work of salvation. This is the evangelical moment. Evangelization is for everyone, and "beautiful upon the mountains are the feet of him who brings glad tidings, announcing salvation."[4]

END NOTES

INTRODUCTION

[1]Luke 24:27, 44-47.
[2]Acts 8:26-40.
[3]*Evangelii Gaudium*, #175.
[4]Evangelii Nuntiandi, #s 14-15.
[5]*The Catechism of the Catholic Church*, #1816.
[6]*Evangelii Gaudium*, #49.
[7]*Ibid.*, #106.

CHAPTER 1

[1]*Evangelii Nuntiandi*, #59; *Evangelium Gaudium*, #s 120-21.
[2]1 Cor. 2:9.
[3]*New York Times*, 2/15//14, A20.
[4]Tim Gunn, "The Day as Masterpiece," *New York Times*, 3/22/15, Metropolitan, p. 2.
[5]*New York Times*, 1/30/12, D2; 1/31/12, B12.
[6]Matt. 21:13.
[7]Ps. 69:8-10, 21.
[8]1 Cor. 4:10.
[9]*The Wanderer*, 1/22/15, 5A.
[10]McCloskey and Shaw, *Good News, Bad News*, 52-53.
[11]Matt. 5:13.

[12]Eph. 5:3-4.

[13]Matt. 7:1; 2 Tim. 2:25.

[14]Prov. 9:8; Sir. 19:12; 20:1.

[15]Matt. 7.

[16]Matt. 7; Titus 3:10; 1 John 5:16.

[17]Luke 17:3; Matt. 18:15-17.

[18]Luke 2:34; John 16:33; Matt. 10:12.

[19]Jer. 1:5; Isaiah 49:15.

[20]Jacobus de Voragine, *The Golden Legend* (Princeton University Press, 1993), II, 102.

[21]Prov. 28:23.

CHAPTER 2

[1]American Family Association *Journal*, May 2015, p. 4.

[2]Gen. 3:21; Ex. 20:26.

[3]Gen. 9:23; Luke 8:27, 35.

[4]John 8:44; 2 Cor. 11:14.

[5]Mark 3:21; Matt. 12:50.

[6]Luke 7:44-46.

[7]Luke 14:1-24.

[8]Warren Carroll, *The Founding of Christendom*, 453.

[9]Rev. 2:6, 14-16, 20.

[10]Carroll, *Founding*, 460.

[11]William Jurgens, ed., *The Faith of the Early Fathers*, I, 25.

[12]Acts 8:20.

[13]Acts 13:10-11.

[14]1 Cor. 5:9-13.

[15]1 Cor. 6:9-11. See also Matt. 24:49; Romans 16-17; 1 Cor. 5:2, 6, 9-13; Gal. 1:9; 2 Tim. 3:2-5; Titus 3:10; 2 John

1:10-11; Prov. 8:16, 20; 19:22, 24-25; 23:20-21; 24:1; Ps. 1:1; 14:3-4; 50:18.

[16]Sir. 12:3; 13:1.

[17]Matt. 10:34-37.

[18]*Evangelium Vitae*, #100.

[19]Matt. 4:2; 6:16; 9:15.

[20]1 Pet. 3:15.

[21]2 Pet. 1:5; 3:17.

CHAPTER 3

[1]*Magnificat* (English version) August 2015, p. 61 (hereafter simply *Magnificat*).

[2]*Pastores Dabo Vobis* (John Paul II's synodal apostolic exhortation of 1992), #33.

[3]*Ibid.*, #47.

[4]George Weigel, *Evangelical Catholicism*, 141.

[5]McCloskey and Shaw, *Good News, Bad News*, 49.

[6]1 Cor. 3:1-2.

[7]Acts 20:27.

[8]Acts 24:25.

[9]*Laudato Si'*, #229.

[10]For Scripture, see Lev. 23:2-3; Heb. 10:25; Matt. 16:18-19.

[11]*Catechism* #1389.

[12]Quoted by Pope Paul VI in his apostolic exhortation of 1975, *Evangelii Nuntiandi*, in maintaining that "the word remains ever relevant, especially when it is the bearer of the power of God" (#42). See also Scott Hahn, *Evangelizing Catholics*, 34 (on Francis).

[13]Mark 1:38.

[14] Matt. 9:37.

[15] Matt. 22:34-40.

[16] Acts 10:42.

[17] *Pastores Gregis*, John Paul II's 2003 post-synodal apostolic exhortation, #29.

[18] *Ibid.*, #31.

[19] Victor Claveau, article on evangelization, *Homiletic and Pastoral Review*, November 2010.

[20] *Pastores Gregis*, #25.

CHAPTER 4

[1] Diane Moczar, *Converts and Kingdoms*, 181.

[2] Luke 9:7-8.

[3] Acts 14:10.

[4] Thackeray, *Josephus*, 98; Luke 7:16; 9:44; Matt. 15:31.

[5] Luke 18:8.

[6] Mal. 3:6; Isaiah 40:8; Ps. 119:151-52.

[7] Matt. 5:18; 24:35; John 10:35.

[8] Heb. 13:8; 2 Tim. 3:16.

[9] Matt. 16:18-19.

[10] G. K. Chesterton, *Orthodoxy*, ch. 3.

[11] Mark 16:16; John 8:24; 1 Cor. 15:17-18.

[12] Acts 18:6.

[13] Acts 13:48.

[14] Acts 4:12.

[15] Hahn, *Evangelizing Catholics*, 38.

[16] John 4:21-24.

[17] Mark 12:27, 34; Matt. 22:34, 46.

[18] Acts 6:8-10; 13:46.

[19] Frederick W. Marks, "The Urgency of Evangelization," *Homiletic and Pastoral Review* (January 2005), pp. 27-28.

[20] Joseph Dirvin, C.M. *Mrs. Seton*, 60.

[21] Frank M. Rega, *St. Francis of Assisi and the Conversion of the Muslims*, 60.

[22] Luke 10:12. See also Mark 16:16; John 8:24; 15:22; 1 Cor. 15:17-18; Matt. 10:15. For the need to listen, see Matt. 13:9; Luke 10:13-16; Acts 3:22-23. For the need to believe after having listened, see Mark 16:16; John 3:18; 15:22. For the need to act on one's belief, see Luke 6:49; Romans 2:6; 1 Cor. 6:9-10; 2 Cor. 5:10; James 2:14; 1 Pet. 1:17; 1 John 2:4.

[23] Avery Dulles, S.J., *The History of Apologetics*, xiii.

[24] Eph. 3:2.

[25] The argument from culture is developed at length in the first chapter of one of my earlier books, *Think and Believe*.

[26] Gal. 6:14.

[27] *Magnificat* (January 2015), 362.

[28] George Weigel, *Evangelical Catholicism*, 144-45.

[29] George Weigel, *Witness to Hope*, 919.

CHAPTER 5

[1] Raymond Arroyo, *Mother Angelica*, 133.

[2] Matt. 16:18-19.

[3] John 21:17.

[4] Compare Matt. 16:18-19 with Isaiah 22:22.

[5] John 10:16; 14:16; 16:13; 17:21.

[6] Acts 4:32.

[7] 2 Pet. 2:1; 1 Cor. 1:10.

[8] 1 Cor. 2:14.

[9] Matt. 19:12; Luke 18:29-30.

[10] Matt. 19:21.

[11] John 15:18-20; Luke 23:31.

[12] Jude 1:7.

[13] Lev. 1:22; 20:13; Deut. 22:5; Rom. 1:32. See also 1 Cor. 6:10.

[14] Matt. 7:6.

[15] Luke 17:1-2.

[16] *Ibid.*

[17] Matt. 7:20.

[18] Quoted by C. John McCloskey III et al., *The Essential Belloc*, 248.

[19] 2 Cor. 3:15-16; 4:4.

[20] Jer. 1:5.

CHAPTER 6

[1] You will find it in the writings of such luminaries as Cardinal Newman and Francis de Sales, as well as in the Council of Trent's Decree on Justification. Going even farther back, it appears in the work of Thomas Aquinas and St. Ambrose (*This Rock*, November 1995, p. 1; *Ambrose Letters*, 1-91 in Fathers of the Church [1954], p. 494). Note how the *Catechism* summarizes Vatican II on the subject: "Those who, through no fault of their own, do not know the Gospel of Christ or his Church, but who nevertheless seek God with a sincere heart, and, moved by grace, try in their actions to do His will as they know it through the dictates of their conscience – these, too, may achieve eternal salvation" (#847).

[2] Acts 10:35; Rom. 2:14.

[3] Matt. 12:41-42.

[4] Matt. 8:10-11.

[5] *New York Times*, 2/24/13, A12.

[6] Pope Francis, *Evangelii Gaudium*, #253.

[7] John L. Allen, *The Global War on Christians*, 203.

[8] For the 75% figure, see the *New York Times*, 12/29/10, A3.

[9] Geisler and Saleeb, *Answering Islam*, 223-25.

[10] Ali and Spencer, *Inside Islam: A Guide for Catholics*, 77.

[11] Curtis Martin, *Made for More*, 34.

[12] E.g. Matt. 4:7; Mark 2:5; 3:12; Luke 10:18; 23:43; John 8:58-59; 10:33.

[13] John 20:17 (italics mine).

[14] William Barclay, *The Gospel of Matthew*, I, 337.

[15] Josephus, Contra Apionem (bk. 1) in L'Estrange, ed. *Works of Flavius Josephus*, vol. 3, p. 277.

[16] Tacitus, *History* 5:5.

[17] Rev. 22:15.

[18] John 19:35; 21:24.

[19] John 17:17-19.

[20] Matt. 16:18-19 (Peter as successor of the Jewish high priest).

[21] Deut. 6:4 and Isaiah 45:18, 21.

[22] Gen. 18:25-27 (Yahweh in the Hebrew).

[23] Gen. 32:31.

[24] Joshua 5:13-15.

[25] Ez. 37:26; Sir. 45:7, 13, 17, 24-25. See also Lev. 24:9.

[26] Ex. 40:32.

[27] Matt. 23:3.

[28] Matt. 5:17-18.

[29] Matt. 19:4.

[30] Matt. 19:12, 29.

[31] Luke 2:41; 4:16.

[32] Ex. 23:4-5; Prov. 25:21.

[33] Acts 2:46.

[34] Num. 6:5; Acts 18:18.

[35] Mal. 1:11.

[36] Matt. 23:15; Acts 2:11.

[37] Robert Sungenis, "Split Personality," *National Review* (April 2009), p. 36.

[38] Sanhedrin 43a, 67a, 104b, 107b.

[39] Sanhedrin 43a.

[40] Yoma 39b, 43c.

[41] Yoma 39a, 39b; Rosh Hashanah, 31b.

[42] Of the forty-six books of the Old Testament, five originated with Moses, and the last six – Ecclesiastes, Sirach, Tobit, 1 and 2 Maccabees, Judith, and Wisdom – were written between the years 300 B.C. and 50 B.C.

[43] John 20:7.

CHAPTER 7

[1] Frank, "The G.O.P.'s Assertive God Squad," *New York Times*, 2/25/15, A23: *Our Sunday Visitor*, 10/19/14, p. 3.

[2] *Merchant of Venice*, III, ii, 73.

[3] Matt. 16:19; 2 Pet. 1:19.

[4] Matt. 19:9.

[5] James 2:24, 26.

[6] Matt. 19:17. See also Matt. 16:27.

[7] 1 Pet. 1:17.

[8] James 1:12.

[9] 2 Tim. 4:14.

[10] Matt. 5:12, 46; 6:2-6, 16-18; 10:42; 25:14-30; Luke 6:35; 14:14.

[11] Matt. 13:21. See also Ez. 18:24-29.

[12] Matt. 24:13.

[13] 2 John 8.

[14] 2 Pet. 1:10; 2:20-22; 3:17.

[15] Phil. 3:12-13; 1 Cor. 9:27; 10:12; 2 Cor. 11:3.

[16] Eph. 2:8-9; 3:28.

[17] Rom. 2:6.

[18] 1Cor. 6:9-10.

[19] Matt. 7:16-21, 24-27; 16:27; 19:17; 25:30, 41-46; Luke 11:28; John 14:21, 23; 15:14. For additional citations that indicate the need for works, see Appendix H.

[20] Luke 3:14.

[21] Matt. 22:21; Luke 7:9.

[22] Luke 22:36-38.

[23] Luke 9:3.

[24] Luke 22:49; John 18:10.

[25] Luke 22:51 (italics mine).

[26] Matt. 26:52.

[27] John 18:11.

[28] See Ed Decker and Dave Hunt, *The God Makers*, 125-26.

[29] See Millet and Akin, "Are the Mormon Scriptures Credible?" *Catholic Answers*, September/October 2012, pp. 21, 23.

[30] See Decker and Hunt, *The God Makers*, 62, 105-107.

[31] *Ibid.*, 114-15.

[32] *New York Times*, 11/11/14, p. A1.

CONCLUSION

[1] 1 Pet. 3:16.

[2] *Il Messaggero*, 6/29/14 reported in *Our Sunday Visitor*, 7/13/14, p. 3.

[3] *National Catholic Register*, 5/19/13, p. 7.
[4] Isaiah 52:7.

APPENDICES

APPENDIX A

PROOF TEXTS

(in small print for use on the street)

Abortion: Jer. 1:5; Isaiah 49:15; Psalm 71:6; Mt. 18:5, 14.

Assumption: If Enoch and Elijah could be assumed into heaven, why not Mary? No city claims her tomb; there are no relics ... See **Tradition**.

Bishops: Phil. 1:1; 1 Tim. 3:1; Titus 1:7. For priests (i.e. "elders" or "presybters," as they were originally called), see Acts 20:17.

Canaanite Slaughter: For Canaanite sodomy, child sacrifice, abortion, witchcraft, cannibalism, etc., as well as God's warning prior to His punishment (i.e. swarms of hornets), see Wisdom 12:4-5, 8-10; Lev. 18:21-27; Ex. 23:21-28; 1 Kings 14:24; 21:26. For God's command, see Dt. 7:1-2, 20. God is sovereign. He can call His sons and daughters home any time He pleases and by whatever means He chooses, whether it be a tsunami, an earthquake, or an Israeli army.

Celibacy and poverty for Church leaders: Mt. 19:12 (eunuchs); Luke 18:29 (leaving wife); 1 Cor. 7:8-9, 32-35, 38. The first generation of priests renounced family life and held all property in common for the good of the community (Acts 2:44-45). The latest research shows that the second generation, though generally married, were expected to live with their wives as brother and sister.

Church Going: for weekly obligation, see Lev. 23:2-3; Heb. 10:25.

Church Organization: Church officials were commissioned, not self-appointed (Acts 14:23; Titus 1;5), with hands laid on them (1 Tim. 4:14); and when they traveled, they were "sent" (Romans 10:14-15). Ignatius, Bishop of Antioch (d. 107 A.D.), speaks in his letters of three distinct levels of ordination: deacons, priests, and bishops.

Confession: John 20:22-23 (Jesus breathes this power on them – the only other time God ever breathed on man was when He breathed life into Adam's nostrils!). It is a life-giving power! And how is a priest to know when to "retain" sins (i.e. when to withhold absolution) unless the sins are confessed to him?

Contraception: Seed-wasting was the sin of Onan and one for which he was struck dead (Gen. 38:9-10). Under the Mosaic Law, capital punishment was not ordained for merely refusing to raise up issue for the wife of a dead brother (Dt. 25:5-10). See also Mt. 19:5 (Man and wife are to be one flesh. How can they be one flesh if they are using contraceptives?). There are also Scriptural passages prohibiting "witchcraft" or "sorcery" – i.e. Gal. 5:20 and Rev. 9:21. The meaning of "witchcraft" or "sorcery" is not what it used to be. During the Middle Ages, the principal stock in trade of witches and sorcerers was contraception and abortion (see Marks, *Think and Believe*, p. 111). *Pharmakeia* in the original Greek means "potions," which was a code word for prophylactics. The earliest Christian conduct book, the *Didaché*, is especially telling in this regard: "You shall not practice magic. You shall not use potions. You shall not procure abortion, nor destroy a new-born child." 20:23, 28.

Divinity of Christ: John 8:58-59 (backed by Ex. 3:14); Matt. 9:2-3; John 20:23, 28.

Divorce: Mt. 5:32; 19:3-9 (use the King James version for Mt. 19). Mk. 10:2-12; Luke 16:18; 1 Cor. 7:10-11.

Eucharist: John 6; Mt. 26:28; 1 Cor. 10:16; 11:23-29. See also 1 Cor. 2:14 for the meaning of "flesh" vs. "spirit" in John 6:64. John 6:63 speaks of the miraculous (which is what the Eucharist is). Ignatius, the martyred bishop of Antioch (d. 107 A.D.) and contemporary of St. John, had a problem with people not coming to Holy Communion. The reason they weren't coming is because they did not believe in the real presence of Jesus in the Eucharist, and his demand that they be shunned is telling (see his letter to the Smyrneans).

Faith vs. Works: That Paul is talking about Jewish hygienic and dietary regulations, as well as circumcision, when he speaks of "works" is evident when one compares the following: Eph. 2:8-9 with Eph. 2:11; Romans 3:28 with 3:29-30; Romans 1:17 and 9:32 with Romans 2:6; Romans 10:12 with Romans 10:9, 13 (one must **do** something!). See also **Works** and **Once Saved**.

"Father": (call no one "father"). We know Jesus did not mean to be taken literally in this instance because He also says (a) "call no one good" (Mark 10:18 and Luke 18:19) and (b) "call no one teacher" (Matt. 23:7-8). He Himself speaks of the "good man who brings forth treasure out of his abundance (Mt. 12:35). See also 1 Pet. 5:13 (Peter speaks of Mark as his son) and Titus 1:4 (Paul calls Titus his son).

Fornication: see **Lists of Mortal Sins.**

Free Will: Gen. 4:7; John 15:22; Mt. 16:16; Sir. 15:15; 21:1. We are never tempted beyond our capacity to resist (1 Cor. 10:13). See also, in this connection, **Once Saved** and **Predestination.**

Graven Images: The verse usually quoted on graven images (Ex. 20:4) is immediately followed by a second verse (Ex. 20:5) which clarifies its meaning. It is the *worshipping* of the images that is wrong (*bowing down* to them in worship), not the having of them. God actually *ordered* the Israelites to fashion graven images (and, as God, He cannot contradict Himself) – see Ex. 25:18 (cherubim over the Ark) and Num. 21:7-9 (bronze serpent).

Hell: mentioned forty times in the New Testament. Tough? Yes. But God's ways are not our ways (Is. 55:8; Ez. 18:29).

Holy Spirit: to be sent to dwell with the Church forever and teach her the truth in its entirety: John 14:16; 16:13.

Jerusalem: to be destroyed and the reason for its destruction: Luke 19:41-44.

Jesus' Mission (reason for coming): atonement and forgiveness of sins (John 3:16; Mt. 26:28; Mark 10:45; Acts 5:31); teaching (Mark 1:38); voluntary atonement (John 10:18).

Immaculate Conception: Genesis 3:15 speaks about God putting "enmity" between Satan and the Woman – this must refer to a special enmity because all of us have a conscience that sets us against evil. The most common objection to the doctrine of the Immaculate Conception is Paul's statement that "all have sinned" (Romans 3:23). But the word "all" need not be taken literally in this case. Jesus did not sin. Paul says that "all" die (1 Cor. 15:22), but Elijah and Enoch were assumed into heaven. Matthew writes that "all" Judea went down to the Jordan to hear John the Baptist (Mt. 3:5). But again, we know that this is not literally true. Two more examples: Mark writes that "all" the disciples swore they wouldn't betray Jesus (Mk. 14:31), but Judas was not on hand to swear. See also the reference to "all" knowledge in Rom. 15:14.

Kneeling: This is the only description we have in Scripture of the prayer posture of (a) Jesus (Luke 22:41), (b) Peter (Acts 9:40), and (c) Paul (Acts 20:36 and 21:5). Eusebius, the first great Church historian (late fourth century), tells us that James, the son of Zebedee and first bishop of Jerusalem, was so often on his knees in prayer that he had callouses on them like those of a camel (*Ecclesiastical History*, V, 5). And he adds, for good measure, that kneeling was the normal praying posture of the early Church (*Ibid.*).

Lists of Mortal Sins: Paul's lists: (a) 1 Cor. 6:9-10; (b) Gal. 5:19-22. Jesus' list: Mt. 15:19.

Mary as Our Queen and Mother: Jesus gave Mary to John (and, by extension, to us) as His mother even as John's biological mother, Salome, stood by watching (Mt. 26:38-44). According to Rev. 12:17, she is the mother of all who keep the Commandments and bear witness to Jesus. She is also described as a queen crowned with twelve stars (Rev. 12:1). The Queen Mother tradition in the Old Testament is especially relevant – next to the king's throne stood the throne of the king's mother (the queen mother), who was expected to have influence with her son. Bathsheba sat enthroned next to Solomon. And this was the pattern with Jewish royals all the way down to the time of Jesus. Question: if God is our father, who is our mother? If Christ is our king, who is our queen?

Mary's Perpetual Virginity: There is no word for "cousin" in Aramaic, the language Jesus spoke. Which explains the use of the word "brother," a catch-all term referring to any close relation. See Galatians 1:19 which speaks of an apostle named James being "the Lord's brother" (there were only two apostles named James, and neither was the son of Mary). We know that Mary had no sexual intercourse with Joseph during pregnancy (Mt. 1:25). The word "until" need not mean what many of our Protestant brethren take it to mean – see 2 Sam 6:23; Dt. 34:6. As for the word "first-born," this was a Jewish expression referring generically to the child that opened the womb (it didn't imply the existence of others – see Ex. 13:2; 34:20; Num. 3:12). If Jesus had brothers and sisters, according to the Protestant interpretation of Mk. 6:3, He must have had at least six. Why do we know nothing of this from Christian tradition, and why would Jesus, impaled on the Cross, entrust Mary to John if His mother had other children – the eldest male being obligated by Jewish law to support his widowed mother. It is also fairly clear that the so-called "brothers" of Jesus who are listed in the Gospel were the sons of another Mary. Compare Mt. 13:55 with Mt. 27:56 in conjunction with John 19:25.

Memory: John 14:26 (the Gospel writers were promised perfect recall by the Lord).

Miracles: promised by Jesus and expected: Mt. 10:1; John 14:12; Acts 4:30.

Mortal sin: see "Lists."

Once Saved: 1 Cor. 10:12; 2 Cor. 11:3; Rom. 11:22; 2 John 8; Ez. 18:24-29. See also the parable of the seed – woe to the one who receives the word immediately with joy but falls away when trouble and persecution come his way (Mt. 13:21); according to Jesus, "he that shall endure [i.e. persevere] to the end will be saved" (Mt. 24:13); Peter's advice: "Give diligence to make your calling and election sure" and "beware lest ye ... fall from your own steadfastness" (2 Pet. 1:10; 3:17); in the same letter, Peter writes: "If, after they have escaped the pollutions of the world through the knowledge of the Lord and Savior Jesus Christ, they are again entangled therein and overcome, the latter end is worse with them than the beginning, for it had been better for them not to have known the way of righteousness, than, after they have known it, to turn from the holy commandment delivered unto them" (2 Pet. 2:20-22). Finally, listen once more to Paul: "Work out your own salvation with fear and trembling"(Phil. 2:12); "I count not myself to have apprehended ... I press toward the mark for the prize of the high calling of God" (i.e. I do not consider that I have laid hold of it already ... I strain forward to what is before [me], I press on towards the goal – Phil. 3:13); I chastise my body and bring it into subjection lest "when I have preached to others, I myself should be a castaway" (i.e. after preaching to others I myself should be rejected" – 1 Cor. 9:27).

Papacy: see **Peter**.

Peter (Petrine Authority): Mt. 16:18-19 (keys given to Peter alone); Luke 22:31-32 (commission to strengthen the brethren given to Peter alone); John 21:15-17 (commission to feed Jesus' lambs, given to Peter alone). Peter pronounces judgment on Paul (2 Pet. 3:16). Paul, in Acts, comes to Jerusalem to consult Peter, not vice versa, on the question of circumcision (Acts 15:2). On the question of papal succession, see Pope Clement I's Letter to the Corinthians which is nothing, if not authoritative in tone (Clement, who was Peter's third successor, died around the year 101 A.D.). Ignatius of Antioch, Irenaeus of Lyons, Ambrose, and Augustine all testified to the primacy of the Roman pontiff.

Pornography: Mt. 5:28.

Predestination: No such thing – see Mt. 18:14; 2 Cor. 5:15; Rom. 8:32; 11:22; 2 Pet. 3:9. One might add something that Jesus said about the Pharisees and lawyers: by failing to go to John for baptism, they brought to naught God's purpose concerning them (Luke 7:30). Finally, there is 1 Tim. 2:4: God wishes "all men to be saved and to come unto the knowledge of the truth."

Purgatory: For Bibles with the deuterocanonical books: 2 Macc. 12:42-46 (80% of the Old Testament quotations contained in the New Testament come from the Septuagint version of Hebrew Scripture [the Greek translation] which included the deuterocanonicals). For Bibles without the deuterocanonicals (like the modern KJB): Rev. 21:27: "There shall in no wise enter into it [heaven] any thing that defileth [i.e. that is unclean]"; 1 Cor. 3:15: "If any man's work shall be burned, he shall suffer loss: but he himself shall be saved; yet so as by fire"; Mt. 12:36: "Every idle word that men shall speak, they shall give account thereof in the day of judgment" (the requirement of an account implies the passing of judgment, and judgment implies punishment). If the opinion of the Church Fathers counts for anything, Augustine and Jerome took Luke 12:59 ("until you have paid the last penny") as a reference to purgatory. One can do the same with Mt. 18:21-35, the parable about the unmerciful servant handed over to the torturers until has paid all he owes ("So, too, will your heavenly father do to you if you do not each forgive …"). Some might argue that Luke 12 and Matthew 18 refer to punishment on earth. But this cannot stand. See Mt. 18:35. And what if a man dies suddenly and painlessly after failing to make just restitution or after acting mercilessly? In 2 Sam. 12:13-14 we read that David had to undergo punishment even though he was forgiven. What if he had died suddenly on the immediate aftermath of repenting? In Luke 12:45-48, servants who misbehave in the absence of their master must endure different degrees of punishment depending on how much they knew about their master's wishes. Again, assuming we are the servants, what if we die before the Lord has punished us? See also 1 Sam. 2:6 where Hannah says that the Lord casts down to the nether world and raises up again? No one emerges from hell where the fire is eternal. So the reference must be to purgatory.

Repetition (i.e. of prayers in the rosary – is it OK?): The objection centers on Jesus' words, "Do not multiply words as the Gentiles do, for they think that by saying a great deal they will be heard" (Mt. 6:7). In the Greek, the word "repetition" never occurs; only "empty words" and "much speaking." The Rosary is not empty words, nor is it much speaking – it takes only fifteen minutes. What Jesus objected to were long-winded wish lists. Simplicity and a spirit of "thy will be done" was what He wanted. In Psalm 136 there are twenty-six repetitions of a single phrase. Jesus repeats Himself three times in prayer (Mt. 26:39-44). And we read in Rev. 4:8 that the four living creatures who are in heaven "do not rest, day and night, saying, "Holy, holy, holy, the Lord God Almighty … .""

Sacraments: Baptism: Mt. 28:19; Confirmation: Acts 8:14-17; Anointing of the Sick: Mark 6:13; James 5:14-16 and Mk. 6:13; Eucharist: John 6; Matt. 26:26-28.

Salvation: *Salvation is from Jesus alone and therefore the Church alone* since the Church is Christ's mystical body – Eph. 5:29-30. Yet, *those outside the Church can be saved* if they fear God and do what is acceptable to him: Acts 10:34-35; Romans 2:10-11, 14-16. Rome has always interpreted the above-cited passages, some of which seem to contradict one another, in such a way as to make them reconcilable. Take, for example, the doctrine of Baptism by desire. No reputable Catholic theologian has ever held that those outside the Church, through no fault of their own, are automatically damned. This would contradict the notion found through the Bible that God is fair and impartial. See, for example, Dt. 10:17; Psalm 98:9; Sir. 35:12; Acts 10:34; Rom. 2:10-11.

Scandals: Luke 17:1.

Scripture as inerrant and timeless: perfect recall of the apostles guaranteed by Jesus (John 14:26); "not one jot or tittle ... . " (Mt. 5:18); Scripture cannot be broken (John 10:35); all of it is useful (2 Tim. 3:16); Jesus: "My words will never pass away" (Mt. 24:35); Jesus Christ is the same yesterday, today, and forever (Heb. 13:8). Luke names 32 countries, 54 cities, 9 islands without a single error of spelling or placement. Does morality change with changing times? "I the Lord do not change" (Mal. 3:6). Isaiah assures us that "the word of our God stands forever" (Isaiah 40:8). Listen, too, to the psalmist addressing the Lord: "All your commands are permanent ... you have established them forever" (Psalm 119:151-52); and again, the Commandments of the Lord are "decreed forever" (Psalm 119:151-52).

Second Coming: 2 Thess. 2:1-3; Mk. 13:32-37.

Sins – Mortal vs. Venial: 1 John 5:16; Ez. 18:24-29; Catechism of the Catholic Church, #2181. See also under "**Lists**" examples of mortal sins.

Sodomy: Genesis, ch.s 18-19 (re: Sodom and Gomorrah); Romans 1:24-32; 1 Cor. 6:9-10; Jude (v. 7).

Suffering: may be offered up for a share in Christ's suffering (Col. 1:24; 1 Pet. 4:13). God will not send us more suffering than we can profitably bear (1 Cor. 10:13).

Temptation: we are never tempted beyond our ability to resist (1 Cor. 10:13).

Tradition: 2 Thess. 2:15 (in the RSV, NAB, Jerusalem translations).

Unity enjoined: Jesus prayed for it at the Last Supper (John 17:20-23); Paul on the need for the Church to be of one mind (1 Cor. 1:10 ff). See also 2 Pet. 2:1.

Websites that are useful:

> www.ewtn.com
> www.catholicanswers.com
> www.jhnetwork.com (for Journey Home Network)

Works Needed (along with faith): James 2:24-26; Mt.16:27; 19:16-21; Romans 2:6; 1 Pet. 1:17; 1 John 2:3; Rev. 20:12. Scriptural lists of sins that keep one from heaven do not include lack of faith: e.g. 1 Cor. 6:9-10; Gal. 5:19-22. In addition to having faith, one must testify to the truth in order to be saved (Rom. 10:10). Testimony (witness/confession) is a work.

APPENDIX B

SIX QUESTIONS FOR JEHOVAH'S WITNESSES

1. **You are pacifists** who say it's wrong to serve as a police officer or soldier. **Yet** Jesus was not a pacifist, and neither was Moses. True, the Ten Commandments tell us we may not kill. But the Hebrew word used by Moses meant "murder" (referring to innocent human beings). One can kill animals – the Jews were ordered to sacrifice lambs in the Temple. The Old Testament is the word of God, but where's the pacifism? Moses commissioned Joshua to take the promised land *by force* and God ordered the extermination of immoral heathen tribes such as the Canaanites. Capital punishment was ordained by God for over a dozen different offenses. Please read the material below for more on this question.

2. **You deny that Jesus was God. Yet,** this is precisely what He claimed to be. Granted, He often spoke as man. But this is because He was BOTH God and man. No other explanation squares with the facts. Jesus told the Jews, "Before Abraham came to be, I am" (John 8:58) – "I am" being the Jewish name for God (Exodus 3:14). Those who heard Jesus' words took up rocks to stone Him because they recognized it for what it was: a claim to divinity. For other evidence that Jesus was God, see the material printed below.

3. **You deny the Real Presence of Jesus in the Eucharist. Yet**, the sixth chapter of the Gospel of John makes clear beyond all reasonable doubt that Jesus gave us His actual body and blood as spiritual food (consumed in our Eucharistic banquet). This was difficult for His listeners to accept. They told Him it was a "hard" saying. It is still hard! But Jesus merely repeated Himself and let "many" of His followers go. Why would the greatest teacher who ever lived let "many" of His students go on the basis of a trivial misunderstanding when He could have cleared it up in four simple words: "Don't take me literally"? **Our Lord, at the Last Supper, took bread in His hands, blessed it, and said, "This is my body." Yet** you've changed the words, as they appear in the original Greek, to read: "This *means* my body." Any Greek scholar with an open mind will agree that this is incorrect. Tampering with the word of God is sacrilegious! See the material printed below for more information.

4. **In order the justify your teaching that evil souls are annihilated at the end of their earthly existence (instead of sent to the eternal fire of hell), your Bible translates the Greek phrase "everlasting fire" as "everlasting cutting off" (Mt. 25:41). No reputable scholar of Greek would agree.**

5. **To justify your teaching that there is more than one god, you translate John 1:1 as "the word [Jesus] was with God and the word was a god" (small "g"). Yet**, the original Greek is indisputably clear. It reads: "the word was with God and the word was God" (capital "G"). How can

there be more than one God when the Bible says plainly that God is one? See Deut. 6:4 and Gal. 3:20.

6. **Your leaders predicted the end of the world in 1914, then again in 1940, and still again in 1975. Yet,** not a single one of these predictions ever borne out. How can such leaders be trusted? The punishment for false prophets in the Bible is death (Deut. 18:20).

MORE ON QUESTION 1

Our Lord told us to "turn the other cheek," but this was meant for individuals, rather than the state. It ruled out things like revenge, vendettas, and hatred in line with Jesus' command to pray for one's enemies. The Master also said, "Render to Caesar the things that are Caesar's" (Matt. 22:21), and people of the time would have regarded taxes and military service as belonging to the state. Peter said, "honor the king" (1 Peter 2:17). Note that the statement is unqualified. Listen also to Paul, "Be subject to princes and authorities, obeying all commands" (Letter to Titus).

WHERE IS PACIFISM IN THE NEW TESTAMENT?

1. John the Baptist, who paved the way for his cousin, Jesus, must have been familiar with Jesus' teachings, and He (John) told soldiers to be content with their pay (Luke 3:14).

2. Jesus exclaimed that He had never seen so much faith in all Israel as He saw in a Roman soldier (Luke 7:1-10).

Nowhere in the Gospel does Jesus outlaw the bearing of arms, and soldiers invariably come off looking good. Peter converted a Roman centurion (Cornelius) who is described as devout and God fearing. The whole tenth chapter of Acts is devoted to this story with nary a hint that Peter told Cornelius to abandon his profession.

3. Our Lord told Peter in the Garden of Gethsemane, "those who live by the sword will die by the sword." But this simply means that one must not take the law into one's own hands (as Peter did when he cut off the ear of the servant of the high priest). Jesus submitted to lawful authority as a matter of principle, but the very purpose of His life was atonement for the sins of mankind, and He wasn't going to let Peter stop Him.

4. There were swords at the Last Supper and Jesus clearly did not object to them (Luke 22:38). Why swords if He was a pacifist?

5. When His disciples asked him in the Garden of Gethsemane, "Shall we strike with the sword?" He replied, "Bear with them [the soldiers sent to arrest him] thus far" (Luke 22:51). Why "thus far" if He was a pacifist?

6. Why, if Jesus was a pacifist, did He say to His disciples at the Last Supper, "let him who has no sword sell his tunic and buy one" (Luke 22:36)? It is sometimes suggested that the swords mentioned at the Last Supper were for protection against wolves and lions. But this will not stand. The apostles had staffs (Luke 9:3), and they had spent years

traversing the countryside where animals would have been far more of a threat than they were in Jerusalem. Why, if Jesus was concerned about physical safety, did He not bring it up at the beginning of His three-year public mission, rather than at the end? It is quite a stretch to assume that protection from animals was on Jesus' mind at the Last Supper.

7.   Pacifism, if Jesus had taught it, would have been a well known doctrine of the early Church. But it is nowhere to be found in the writings of the early Christians, who refused to serve in the Roman army because every soldier had to take an oath of allegiance to the **emperor as God**.

MORE ON QUESTION 2:
THE CASE FOR CHRIST'S DIVINITY

1.   Jesus told His followers, "Before Abraham came to be, I am" (John 8:58). This is significant because "I am" was the Hebrew term for God (Ex. 3:14). Jehovah's Witnesses have changed "I am" to "I have been," which is an incorrect rendering of the original Greek. When Jesus' listeners heard these words, they picked up rocks to stone Him to death because they grasped what readers of the Jehovah's Witness Bible are sure to miss: He was claiming to be God!

2.   Jesus spoke of the glory He had with the Father before the world existed and claimed that the Father loved Him before the creation of the world (John 17:5 and 24).

3.   Jesus claimed to be able to forgive sins, something only God can do (Matt. 9:3).

4.   Many times, Jesus referred to Himself as "the son of God" in the sense of being co-equal with the Father, and Jewish leaders were quite clear about what He was claiming (divinity). See Matt. 26:62-66; John 5:18; 9:35-38; 10:22-39.

5.   When Thomas saw the risen Lord, he said, "My Lord and **my God**," and Jesus did not object (John 20:28).

6.   John begins his Gospel, "In the beginning was the Word [referring to Christ] and the Word was with God, and the Word was God" (John 1:1-7). Jehovah's Witness Bibles change the phrase "was God" to "was **a God**." But this is an incorrect rendering of the original Greek.

7.   Jesus said that "all things that the Father has are mine" (John 16:15). Another claim to equality with the Father.

MORE ON QUESTION 3:
THE CASE FOR THE EUCHARIST

1.   Jesus told His followers that "unless you eat the flesh of the Son of Man and drink his blood, you shall not have life in you … . for my flesh is food indeed and my blood is drink indeed" (John 6:51-57). This came after the miraculous multiplication of loaves (verses 1-15), and many of Jesus' followers, upon hearing it, wanted to leave Him. "This is a hard saying!" they told Him (John 6:61). But Jesus stood

his ground, refusing to qualify his language. "Does this scandalize you?" He asked, comparing the Eucharist to the miracle of His Ascension (John 6:63). After repeating Himself three times, He let the protesters go, and so far as we know, they never returned (verses 61-67). How likely is it that the world's greatest teacher would let "many" of his disciples go on the basis of a simple misunderstanding – one that could have been eliminated with the utterance of four words, "Don't take me literally"? Notice, too, that the problem was not one of misunderstanding. Rather, as John points out, it was one of belief (verses 65 and 70). They could not or would not **believe**. People still refuse to believe!

2. Those who deny the Real Presence of Christ in the Eucharist should reread John 6, paying particular attention to verses 63-64, wherein Jesus warns that the Eucharist cannot be understood except through the medium of the "spirit." Those who were of the flesh took Jesus' words as a reference to cannibalism because they couldn't or wouldn't believe the God-Man capable of giving His flesh and blood without being, in some way, diminished. Paul, in his first letter to the Corinthians, puts his finger on the underlying problem: "The sensual man does not perceive the things that are of God."

3. At the Last Supper, Jesus did not say, "This bread is to be a memorial" or "This bread is a symbol of my body." What He said was, "This IS my body ... This IS my blood" (Matt. 26:26-28). See also Mark 14:22-24; Luke 22:19-20.

4. St. Paul, writing about the need to eat the bread and drink the cup, warned that if any member of the congregation ate unworthily he or she would be guilty of Christ's body and blood (1 Cor. 11:23-28). In other words, the Eucharist was no ordinary meal.

5. We also have the testimony of St. Ignatius, martyred Bishop of Antioch (c. 110 A.D.) and a contemporary of St. John, who wrote, on the way to martyrdom: "The Eucharist is the flesh of our Savior Jesus Christ." Ignatius had nothing but harsh criticism for Christians who absented themselves from Holy Communion, maintaining that they should be shunned because "they do not confess that the Eucharist is the Flesh of our Savior Jesus Christ" (Letter to the Smyrnaeans).

6. Justin Martyr, who ran the Christian school of apologetics in Rome, wrote around year 145 A.D.: "The Eucharist ... is both the flesh and blood of Jesus."

7. All the Fathers of the Church, including Augustine, are as one on this subject.

MORE ON QUESTION 6:
FALSE WITNESS

The Bible describes a true prophet of God as one who never makes a false prediction (Deut. 18:20-22; 1 Kings 17:24). This is important because the founder of the Witnesses, a man named Charles Taze Russell, predicted that the Second Coming of Christ would occur in 1914. When it didn't happen, Russell alleged that Jesus had come "invisibly" and would "soon return in a more visible manner." Russell died in 1916 without witnessing a coming of any kind, but his unfulfilled predictions did not deter his successor, Joseph Rutherford, from forecasting a landing in southern California in 1925 of Abraham, Isaac, Jacob, and the prophets.

Rutherford, who died in 1942, was succeeded by Nathan Homer Knorr, who held that Armageddon would occur in 1975. When this didn't happen, Knorr's replacement, Frederick Franz said that the end was not far off. Finally, Milton Henschel, his successor as head of the Witnesses, altered church doctrine to state that the end would be "soon." In the Old Testament, God ordered false prophets killed (Deut. 18:20). Jesus Himself was very clear: "As for the exact day or hour, no one knows it, neither the angels in heaven nor the Son, but the Father only... . You cannot know the day your Lord is coming... . The Son of Man is coming at a time you least expect" (Matt. 24:36, 42, 44). Time and again, the leaders of the JWs have been wrong in their predictions. What is the logical conclusion?

CELEBRATION OF CHRISTMAS

You are right when you say that nowhere in Scripture does Jesus command us to celebrate his birth. Equally true: the Bible does not give us December 25 as the date of the Nativity. But, according to Matthew 16:18-19, Jesus gave Peter **complete authority** over the Church, and history indicates that this petrine authority was passed on to successors (just as the high priesthood continued on down through the centuries before Christ). If the head of the Church wants a celebration of Christ's birth, he can have it. He can also pick the day.

In the eyes of JWs, Christmas is depressingly commercial. There is too much pressure to shop and socialize. There may be some truth in this. But it's up to the individual to avoid commercialization by buying off season or reducing the number of gifts. As for socialization, it can be adjusted and controlled.

Are we supposed to eliminate Thanksgiving because (a) cooking for a crowd can be burdensome, (b) folks tend to overeat, and (c) we may not feel comfortable with the social mix? Once again, it's up to the individual to find a way around such problems. Why throw the baby out with the bath water? Christmas is beautiful, an awesome season of light! December would be dark without the Nativity. Jesus' birth changed the world for the better, and it's the basis for our calendar!

USE OF THE WORD "JEHOVAH"

Jehovah's Witnesses claim that the Old Testament books found in Catholic Bibles are flawed because the Jewish word "Jehovah" has been replaced with "God" or "Lord." First of all, modern scholars believe "Yahweh" comes closer than "Jehovah" to the way the Jews of old would have pronounced the name of God, and there are Bibles that actually use "Yahweh" (e.g. the Jerusalem Bible, an excellent scholarly French version dating to the 1960s and translated into English). Secondly, and more importantly, the Septuagint or Greek version of Hebrew Scripture, which was the one favored by Jesus and his apostles (80% of the Old Testament references found in it are taken from the Septuagint) used "Lord," instead of "Yahweh" or "Jehovah." If it was good enough for Jesus, it should be good enough for us.

APPENDIX C

FATIMA: THE GREATEST MIRACLE OF OUR TIME

On October 13, 1917 in the Portuguese village of Fatima, there occurred a miracle that can only be described as the most stunning event of modern times because it was witnessed by an estimated 70,000 people, atheists included; also because the facts in question were acknowledged by Portugal's anti-clerical press.

The Story

What happened may be simply told. On May 13, 1917, three children aged 7, 9, and 10 came home after pasturing their sheep and reported that Mary, the mother of Jesus, had appeared to them, urging prayer and mortification in reparation for sin. She had said additionally that she would return on the 13th day of each succeeding month and work a great miracle on October 13 so "that all may believe."

The Circumstances

The faith of the Portuguese people was under heavy siege at this time because their government had fallen into the hands of totalitarian leftists. Priests and nuns had been jailed. Celebration of the Mass had been severely restricted to the point where it was practically extinct in urban areas. Portugal was well on its way to becoming the first Communist state.

Mary Keeps Her Word

The Blessed Mother came every month, as promised, and though she was not seen by the vast majority of onlookers, she manifested her presence in ways that were subtly suggestive. Some of the bystanders saw a cloud formation that resembled the burning of incense. Others saw rainbow colors, along with a luminous globe in a cloudless sky. On one occasion, there was a flash, on another a faint buzzing sound. Witnesses told of hearing the roll of thunder in fair weather. There was reference as well to the sight of glittering gossamer and flower petals falling from heaven. Lucia's radiance was again telling. She positively glowed with rapture during the apparitions, bringing more and more people to her side. On June 13 the crowd was estimated at 500, and by July 13, the number had risen to 2,000. By October 13, the day of the miracle, 70,000 had come from near and far. Agnostics, hard-bitten journalists, and anti-clerical officials – all were there awaiting what they all expected would be a non-event.

The First Miracle

It rained long and hard the night before October 13 – so hard that many were soaked to the bone. Around 1 PM on the 13th, Lucia called out: "Put down your umbrellas!" and many did so in spite of the downpour. Suddenly, as if by magic, everyone was dry as a bone. Scientists tell us that the amount of energy required to dry the clothes of 70,000 spectators instantaneously should have killed all present.

The Miracle of the Sun

With everyone comfortably dry, the sun, after spinning rapidly and throwing off a variety of colors, appeared to zigzag and hurtle at tremendous speed toward the earth, causing many to fall to the ground. Some fainted. Others wept as objects turned all colors of the rainbow. Eyewitnesses also testified that they had been able to look directly at a sun shining unfiltered against a background of blue sky.

Press Reports

On October 15, the anti-clerical, Masonic editor of Portugal's most popular newspaper, *O Seculo*, published an account of what he called "a spectacle unique and incredible" in which the sun resembled "a silver plate." "One would say that an eclipse had occurred," he wrote, describing the crowd as "pale with fear" and the sun as trembling, making "abrupt movements never seen before and outside all cosmic laws." Two days later, on October 17, *O Dia*, the Portuguese paper with the second highest circulation, published a second account that dovetailed neatly with the first: "the silver sun ... [was] seen to whirl ... people fell on their knees ... the light turned to a beautiful blue." Eventually, hundreds of eyewitness were interviewed. Some of them had observed the miracle from as far away as 40 kilometers, and the recollections, which were in substantial agreement, have since been published. An atheist on the faculty of Columbia University wrote a vivid description of the miracle, and there is a massive volume in Portuguese containing a treasure trove of information yet to be translated into English.

The Credibility of the Children

The credibility of the children is, of course, great owing to the miracle itself. But there is the added fact that Lucia had to face angry, unbelieving parents, as well as a skeptical pastor who didn't want trouble from the state. Added to this, secular authorities used every ruse and threat they could devise to get the children to retract their story. After abducting them on August 13 to head off another meeting with Mary, they threatened to throw them into a cauldron of boiling oil unless they changed their tune. They were then separated and each told that the other two had undergone martyrdom. Again, they hued to their line, risking a cruel death. In the end, they wound up in jail with hardened criminals, some of whom, seeing them fall on their knees in prayer, did the same out of sympathy. One of them was even converted!

What They Endured

Photographs taken of the youngsters show them looking unhappy and scared. Small wonder. Their parents were in anguish during their incarceration not knowing their whereabouts. Their very lives hung in the balance, not only then, but later when anti-clericals kept insisting that the miracle of the sun had been invented, that simple people had been deceived by means of collective suggestion. Furious, too, at the thought of a religious groundswell, they did all in their power to block Fatima processions, going so far as to use violence. Freemasons placed four bombs in the Fatima chapel and a fifth by the holm oak where Our Lady had appeared. The tree bomb failed to explode, but the chapel roof was blown off, and so great was the tension that Lucia had to leave town.

Two Other Reasons

Two other reasons for crediting the children stem from things reported long before October 13. First, after meeting the Virgin on July 13, they quoted her as having said that without prayer and mortification, Russia would fall into error and spread lies around the world. Nations would be destroyed (this was more than three months before October 20 when Lenin left his hideaway hut in Finland to launch the Russian Revolution). Secondly, the children mentioned a promise from Mary that, in answer to their request, two out of the three seers would soon join her in heaven (a flu epidemic at the end of the decade took the life of Jacinta and Francisco, but Lucia lived to be almost a hundred).

One Last Reason

A final factor in the "belief equation" is the fact that Lucia and her two cousins were remarkably mature from a spiritual standpoint. No ordinary children, they prayed the rosary in the fields prior to 1917 and mortified themselves in any number of ways. They fasted. They abstained from water. They wore coarse rope around their waist next to the skin – all in response, they maintained, to the prompting of three angels who appeared to them in the summer of 1916. The angels had taught them how to pray and, at the same time, informed them of the need to embrace suffering for the sake of its redemptive value.

Conclusion

Fatima is, far and away, the most thoroughly authenticated miracle since the Resurrection of Christ. Along with Lourdes, It is also the best known, and what is interesting about Lourdes and Fatima is what they have in common. In both cases, the Blessed Mother appeared to Catholics, and both miracles remind us of things recounted in Scripture. Fatima harks back to the miracles of the sun witnessed by Joshua (Josh. 10) and Hezekiah (1 Kings 20), while Lourdes is a replay of what transpired at the Pool of Bethesda when a man was cured by wading into water stirred by an angel (John 5). Those who find it hard to believe in biblical inerrancy will find their faith strengthened by modern-day miracles. Conversely, those inclined to doubt the testimony of the Fatima children will be moved to believe by what they find in Sacred Scripture.

The Big Picture

In the final analysis, Fatima is much more than a miracle. It is many miracles rolled into one. We think of the miracle of the sun, something undeniably wondrous. But just as wondrous as the event itself is the fact that it was predicted three months in advance – to the exact day – by children. In the case of the predictions that forecast when Jacinta and Francisco would die and what would happen to Russia, they are again miraculous because in both cases, the outcomes were highly unlikely. The joy and enthusiasm with which children as young as Lucia, Jacinta, and Francisco embraced prayer and penance is again awesome. Last of all, the fact that the children were strong enough psychologically to adhere to their story in the face of bitter opposition from naysaying parents, incredulous church officials, and hostile civil authorities is again nothing short of marvelous.

Endnote

It should perhaps be added that Fatima is the name of Mohammed's daughter, said by Muslims to have given birth virginally. It is also the name of the Portuguese convert from Islam to Christianity whose name was given to the town in Portugal where the miracle of the sun took place. For further reading, see John De Marchi, *Fatima from the Beginning* (Fatima: Missoes Consolata, 2002), which contains photos of newspaper articles; also Louis Kondor, ed., *Fatima in Lucia's Own Words: Sister Lucia's Memoirs* (Fatima: Secretariado dos Pastorinhos, 2003); William Thomas Walsh, *Our Lady of Fatima* (Garden City, New York: Doubleday, 1954); and John Young, "The Importance of Fatima," *Homiletic and Pastoral Review* (August/September 2000). For interviews of hundreds of eyewitnesses, see John Haffert, *Meet the Witnesses* (Spring Grove, Pennsylvania: American Society for the Defense of Tradition, Family, and Property, 2006).

APPENDIX D

MESSIANIC PROPHECY
IN JEWISH SCRIPTURE
POINTS TO JESUS

Old Testament "Suffering Servant" Predictions (regarding the manner in which Jesus would suffer and die):

1. He would be scourged. Compare Isaiah 50:6 and 53:5 with Matt. 27:26.
2. He would be mocked. Compare Psalm 22:7-8 with Matt. 27:29.
3. He would be spat upon. Compare Isaiah 50:6 with Matt. 27:30.
4. He would be wounded in the hands and feet. Compare Psalm 22:17 and Isaiah 53:5 with John 19:18 and 20:27.
5. He would be pierced through the heart. Compare Psalm 109:22 and Zechariah 12:10 with John 19:34.
6. Not a bone of his body would be broken (contrary to the usual practice of breaking legs when crucifixion was cut short). Compare Psalm 34:21 with John 19:33.
7. He would be counted among the wicked. Compare Isaiah 53:12 with Matt. 27:38.
8. His executioners would cast lots for His clothing. Compare Psalm 22:19 with Matt. 27:35.
9. He would not undergo corruption (Psalm 16:10).

Other Messianic Prophecies:

10. He would be called God. See Isaiah 7:14 and 9:5 (Immanuel means "God with us").
11. He would be born in Bethlehem (Micah 5:1).
12. He would be born of a virgin (Isaiah 7:14).
13. His betrayer would receive thirty pieces of silver. Compare Zechariah 11:13 with Matt. 27:3.
14. He would come from the tribe of Judah (Genesis 49:10), in particular from Jesse and David (Isaiah 7:13-14; 2 Samuel 7:12).
15. He would rule "by the rod of His mouth" (i.e. non-violently). See Isaiah 11:4.
16. He would be a light to the Gentiles and to the ends of the earth. See Isaiah 49:6.
17. He would inaugurate a universal priesthood of the laity (i.e. all would have access to the Holy of Holies). See Isaiah 61:6.
18. The Aaronic priesthood would never pass away (Sirach 45:13).
19. God's sanctuary would last forever (Ezekiel 37:26).

According to an expert on Jewish history, rabbis at the time of Christ's birth had identified 456 passages in the Old Testament that described the coming of the long-expected Messiah. The chance that one of these prophecies would be fulfilled in Christ was slight. Take, for example, the prediction that He would be a direct descendant in the male line of King David (chances: one in a hundred). Abraham Lincoln had four children; yet there are no male descendants of Lincoln alive today that carry the family name. The chance that two prophesies would be fulfilled in Christ is perhaps one in a thousand. The chance that anyone would fulfill every single one of the prophecies, as Christ did, has been estimated as one in 8,400,00,000,000,000,000,000,000,000.

APPENDIX E

LETTER TO A LAPSED CATHOLIC

Dear Brett,

It was a pleasure chatting with you at the CVRTL dinner. I was fascinated by all you had to say and wish you nothing but the best. I worry, though, about your exit from the Catholic Church, well intentioned as it may have been. Our Church is not perfect, composed, as it is, of fallible human beings. Even the Pope is fallible when it comes to matters of politics, economics, and discipline. Only when he speaks on faith and morals to the entire Church is he safeguarded by the Holy Spirit.

You said you don't think it matters what church we belong to as long as we keep the Ten Commandments. But: (1) who is to say what is included under the rubric of the Ten Commandments? Do they tell us what to think of remarriage after divorce? Abortion? Contraception? Euthanasia? Fornication? Same-sex "marriage"? I could go on and on. (2) It is for this very reason that Jesus set up a church led by a single individual, Peter, with absolute power to bind and loose on matters of faith and morals – a single individual specially guided by the Holy Spirit on hot button issues. In the Gospel of Matthew, we learn that Jesus gave this power to Peter alone (he is the only one given the keys to the kingdom). In the Gospel of John, we learn that Jesus promised to send the Holy Spirit, the spirit of truth, to lead his church to the fullness of truth and never to abandon it.

Why is the Catholic Church the only one that stands rock-like on the key moral issues of our time – against all tides of opinion, all fads, all politically correct theory? How has it managed to remain true to early Christian values for two thousand years? Could it have been wrong in its teaching on such important topics as the Real Presence of Jesus in the Eucharist and Papal Infallibility for 1500 years with the Holy Spirit guiding it? It was not until 1500 years into its history that Protestant reformers came up with the idea that important teachings such as these were mistaken!

By now, I imagine you've read and meditated on the sixth chapter of John's Gospel. So I ask you: is it really conceivable that the world's greatest teacher would willingly let many of His students leave Him on the basis of a trivial misunderstanding? It is the job of the teacher to clarify when there is doubt. NOWHERE in the Gospels is Jesus ever asked to explain one of His sayings that He does not oblige.

This is only one example of how the Catholic interpretation of Scripture *makes sense*! There are hundreds of others. But I don't wish to try your patience. Come on back! Come back to the Church! The sacrament of Reconciliation is superior to anything a psychiatrist could ever offer you, and it is free. All you need is the resolve to change your life, along with a willingness to admit you're not perfect and the humility to accept whatever penance you may be given by the priest who stands in for Jesus. Many of our churches are open all day for visits before the Blessed Sacrament. Holy Communion alone is a privilege that far outweighs any loss of respect that you could ever suffer for a return to Catholicism. I'm sure you know that the earliest Christians were not well respected either! Their lives were sought by Jews and Romans alike! We were born to seek the truth and then to embrace it at all costs. So do it! You'll never regret it.

If you'd like to discuss these or any other issues connected with the Faith, call me at my home. If I'm not in, I'll return your call and we can talk.

God bless.

Yours truly,

APPENDIX F

RECOMMENDED READING

(a sampling to whet the appetite)

REFERENCE WORKS

William Jurgens, *The Faith of the Early Fathers* (3 vols.) – writings of the Church Fathers, especially vol. 1.

Catholic Encyclopedia.

Butler's *Lives of the Saints* (4 vols.)

Harper's Bible Dictionary.

William Barclay's commentary on the books of the New Testament

Inside the Bible by Kenneth Baker, S.J. (an introduction to each book of the Bible).

The Interlinear NIV: Parallel New Testament in Greek and English by Alfred Marshall.

Gleason Archer, *Encyclopedia of Bible Difficulties.*

APOLOGETICS

Mere Christianity by C. S. Lewis

Rome Sweet Home by Kimberly and Scott Hahn

Catholicism and Fundamentalism by Karl Keating

What Catholics Really Believe by Karl Keating

Born Fundamentalist, Born Again Catholic by David Currie

Catholic Street Evangelization edited by Steve Dawson

The Case for Christ by Lee Strobel

Radio Replies by Rumble and Carty (3 vols.)

Free from All Error by William Most

Apologetics Today by William Most

Catholicism and Reason by Hayes, Hayes, and Drummey

Who Do You Say That I Am by James Drummey

The Faith of Our Fathers by James Cardinal Gibbons

The Bible and Birth Control by Charles Provan

Think and Believe by Frederick Marks

Pope Fiction by Patrick Madrid

Christianity on Trial by Vincent Carroll and David Shiflett

What's So Great About Christianity by Dinesh D'Souza

In Defense of Miracles by Douglas Geivett and Gary R. Habermas

Celibacy in the Early Church by Stefan Heid

Answering Islam by Norman Geisler and Abdul Saleeb

CATECHESIS

The Bible

The Child's Story Bible by Catherine F. Vos (for the Old Testament)

Illustrated Bible History of the Old and New Testaments by Ignatius Schuster

Catechism of the Catholic Church

Fundamentals of Catholic Dogma by Ludwig Ott

The Essential Catholic Survival Guide by the staff of Catholic Answers

Right and Reason by Austin Fagothey, S.J.

The Mark of Holiness by Robert D. Smith

HISTORY

The History of the Church by Eusebius (the first of the great
  Church historians covers the first three centuries)
Christ the King, Lord of History by Anne Carroll
A History of Christendom by Warren Carroll (6 vols.), especially
  vol. 1.
How the Reformation Happened by Hilaire Belloc
Characters of the Reformation by Hilaire Belloc
The Great Heresies by Hilaire Belloc
God's Battalions: The Case for the Crusades by Rodney Stark
Galileo by David Wooten
Philip II by William Thomas Walsh
The Spanish Inquisition: A Historical Revision by Henry Kamen
Comparative Miracles by Robert D. Smith
Marvels of Charity: History of American Sisters and Nuns by
  George C. Stewart, Jr.
The Last Crusade by Warren Carroll (the Spanish Civil War)
1917: Red Banners White Mantle by Warren Carroll
The Thirteenth Greatest of Centuries by James J. Walsh
Those Terrible Middle Ages by Régine Pernoud

DEVOTIONAL

The Imitation of Christ by Thomas à Kempis
Introduction to the Devout Life by St. Francis de Sales
The Spiritual Exercises of St. Ignatius of Loyola
Words in Pain by Bishop John Wright (for Lent)
The Way by Josemaría Escrivá

Journeys Home edited by Marcus Grodi (3 volumes) – stories of converts

The Greatest Story Ever Told by Fulton Sheen

The Incorruptibles by Joan Carroll Crux

Hope for the Troubled Heart by Billy Graham

Our Lady of Fatima by William Thomas Walsh

The Many Faces of Virtue by Donald DeMarco

Healing Fire of Christ: Reflections on Modern Miracles by Paul Glynn

LIVES OF THE SAINTLY

Secrets of the Saints by Henri Ghéon (especially the first section on the Curé D'Ars)

Born for Friendship by Bernard Basset

Saint John Fisher by Michael Davies

Damien the Leper by John Farrow

Dominican Saints by Dominican Novices

Saint-Watching by Phillis McGinley

Saint Edmund Campion by Evelyn Waugh

St. Paul by Daniel-Rops

St. Francis of Assisi by Johannes Jörgensen

Saint Anthony the Wonder-Worker of Padua by Charles Warren Stoddard

Maria Chapdelaine by Louis Hémon

St. Isaac and the Indians by Milton Lomask

A Man for Others by Patricia Treece (the life of Maximilian Kolbe)

Give Me Souls by Peter Lappin (the life of Don Bosco)

Mrs. Seton by Joseph Dirvin, C.M.

Treasure in Clay by Fulton Sheen (his autobiography)

Mother Angelica by Raymond Arroyo

Faithful for Life: The Autobiography of Father Paul Marx, O.S.B.

G. K. Chesterton by Ian Kerr

APPENDIX G

David Copperfield (1934)

Scrooge (1935)

Tale of Two Cities (1935)

Fury (1936)

Little Lord Fauntleroy (1936)

The Story of Louis Pasteur (1936)

Captains Courageous (1937)

The Prince and the Pauper (1937)

Angels with Dirty Faces (1938)

Boy's Town (1938)

The Citadel (1938)

You Can't Take It With You (1938)

Holiday (1938)

Dodge City (1939)

Gone with the Wind (1939)

Mr. Smith Goes to Washington (1939)

The Wizard of Oz (1939)

The Fighting 69th (1940) – war movie

Edison the Man (1940)

Shop Around the Corner (1940)

Knute Rockne, All American (1940)

Abe Lincoln in Illinois (1940)

Night Train to Munich (1940)

Sergeant York (1941)

Hold Back the Dawn (1941)

Meet John Doe (1941)

Blossoms in the Dust (1941)

Casablanca (1942)

Saboteur (1942)

Shadow of a Doubt (1943)

Lassie Comes Home (1943)

Double Indemnity (1944)

The Keys of the Kingdom (1944)

National Velvet (1944)

The Bells of St. Mary's (1945)

A Song to Remember (1945)

Mildred Pierce (1945)

Henry V (1945)

Destry Rides Again (1946)

It's A Wonderful Life (1946)

Great Expectations (1946)

Johnny Belinda (1948) – caution: momentary sexual assault.

I Remember Mama (1948)

Joan of Arc (1948)

Oliver Twist (1948)

Treasure of the Sierra Madre (1948)

Miracle of the Bells (1948)

The Heiress (1949)

Kind Hearts and Coronets (1949)

Madame Bovary (1949) – perfectly clean

Quartet (1949)

Come to the Stable (1949)

Asphalt Jungle (1950)

Harvey (1950)

Last Holiday (1950)

The Gunfighter (1950)

African Queen (1951)
The Great Caruso (1951)
The Lavender Hill Mob (1951)
Christmas Carol (1951)
Cry the Beloved Country (1951)
The Man in the White Suit (1951)
Major Barbara (1952)
High Noon (1951)
Miracle of Our Lady of Fatima (1952)
The Steel Trap (1952)
The Robe (1953)
Captain's Paradise (1953)
The Magnificent Obsession (1954)
Blackboard Jungle (1955)
The Ladykillers (1955)
Marty (1955)
Oklahoma (1955)
The Catered Affair (1956)
Giant (1956)
The King and I (1956)
The Man Who Knew Too Much (1956)
The Ten Commandments (1956)
The Lone Ranger – Hi Yo Silver (1956) – western
An Affair to Remember (1957)
Bridge on the River Kwai (1957)
Twelve Angry Men (1957)
Witness for the Prosecution (1957)
Heaven Knows, Mr. Alison (1957)
The Bravados (1958) – caution: momentary sexual assault.
Big Country (1958) – caution: momentary sexual assault.
Ben Hur (1959)

Diary of Anne Frank (1959)

The FBI Story (1959)

Last Train to Gun Hill (1959) – caution: momentary sexual assault.

Pollyanna (1960) despite implicit criticism of hell-fire preaching

The Guns of Navarone (1961)

The Hoodlum Priest (1961)

Pocketful of Miracles (1961)

The Miracle Worker (1962)

The Man Who Shot Liberty Valance (1962)

Lawrence of Arabia (1962)

Lilies of the Field (1963)

Mary Poppins (1964)

My Fair Lady (1964)

The Sound of Music (1965)

Shenandoah (1965)

Patch of Blue (1965)

Man for All Seasons (1966)

To Sir with Love (1967)

True Grit (1969)

Chisum (1970)

Sounder (1972)

Murder on the Orient Express (1974)

The Man Who Would be King (1975)

Enemy of the People (1977)

Les Miserables (1978 – by far the best version)

A Time for Miracles (1980)

Chariots of Fire (1981)

Gandhi (1982)

The Scarlet and the Black (1983)

Anne of Green Gables (1985)

Silverado (1985)

Hoosiers (1986)

Stand and Deliver (1987)

Babette's Feast (1987)

Bernadette (1988)

Glory (1989)

Lean on Me (1989)

My Name is Bill W. (1989)

Driving Miss Daisy (1989)

The Jeweler's Shop (1990)

The Pistol (1990)

Enchanted April (1991)

Mrs. Arris Goes to Paris (1992)

Don Bosco (1993)

Remains of the Day (1993)

Little Women (1994)

Persuasion (1995)

Mr. Holland's Opus (1995)

Sense and Sensibility (1995)

Emma (1996)

Jane Eyre (1996)

In This House of Brede (1997)

Mansfield Park (1999)

The Simple Life of Noah Dearborn (1999)

October Sky (1999)

The Winslow Boy (1999)

Second Hand Lions (2003)

The Passion of the Christ (2004) in spite of a prolonged and
    graphic interlude of torture

The Passion of Bernadette (2006)

Akeelah and the Bee (2006)

The Pursuit of Happiness (2006)

Miss Potter (2007)

Bella (2007)

Flash of Genius (2008)

Fireproof (2008)

Little Dorrit (2009 – BBC TV)

Bleak House (2009 – BBC TV)

The Last Brickmaker in America (2010)

Saint Giuseppe Moscati: Doctor of the Poor (2012)

Courageous (2012)

October Baby (2012)

God's Not Dead (2014)

Nudity on the silver screen has found defenders among a number of Catholic film critics, who point to Michelangelo's work, along with the kind of art found in Old World churches, as proof of a permissive Christian tradition. It is interesting, though, that John Paul II, in his *Theology of the Body* (1997), finds a "very important difference" between cinema and classical art that "contained an element of sublimation" (p. 227). How can one compare cinema with the work of Michelangelo when the latter is idealized, stationery, and silent? In the second place, it is far easier to turn away from a risqué painting than to walk out on a film.

Some claim that "redeeming themes" justify objectionable content, and a 1995 Vatican list of "great" pictures has been cited for its inclusion of *The Mission* and *Schindler's List*, both of which show frontal nudity. As for redeeming themes, St. John Bosco asked, "Would you drink something you knew was poisoned just because it was offered to you in a golden cup?"

(Johnston, ed., *Voice*, p. 12). The "golden cup," in this case, being a redeeming theme. The end does not justify the means.

As for Vatican lists, they are not infallible. *Schindler's List* stands condemned by orthodox rabbis in spite of a strong pro-Jewish message, while *The Mission* is objectionable not only for its exploitation of female nudity, but also because it falsifies history in such a way as to bring the papacy into contempt (Madrid, *Pope Fiction*, 199-201).

There are always those who claim that frontal nudity is not a problem for "most reasonable viewers." But where is the evidence? St. Philip Neri warns: "In the matter of purity there is no greater danger than not fearing danger. When a person puts himself in an occasion [of sin] and says, 'I shall not fall,' it is an almost infallible sign that he will fall, and with great injury to his soul" (Johnston, *The Voice of the Saints*, 1965, p. 61). Pope Paul VI, in *Humanae Vitae*, spoke of the "need to create a climate favorable to chastity."

In the last analysis, a man must ask himself whether he would want his wife or daughter exposed before the eye of a cameraman. If the answer is no, how can he support the exploitation of someone else's wife or daughter? To quote *The Theology of the Body* again, the "right to privacy" is violated when the "rules of the gift [of self to spouse] and of mutual donation … are violated" (p. 223).

There are those who argue that violence in the movies is as objectionable as graphic sex. But again, this will not stand. Violence of the wrong kind may be harmful, but it is not as debilitating as graphic sexual content which enslaves because it is as addictive as crack or cocaine. Scientific findings bear out the fact that pornography has deleterious, long-term biochemical effects on the brain (*National Catholic Register*, December 12-18, 2004, pp. 1, 10).

What we need is a revival of the standards that prevailed during the golden age of Hollywood (1937-57) when public taste was molded by the Legion of Decency. Such a revival may seem unlikely at the moment, but we must do our part to bring it about, and if we are asked to recommend classic films that are devoid of nudity, we should be ready with a list.

APPENDIX H

ADDITIONAL "WORKS" PROOF TEXTS

1. St. John warns us that we can't even *know* the Lord unless we keep His commandments (1 John 2:3). Neither can we abide in His love without doing so (John 15:10) or be His friends (John 15: 14).

2. Why is Tabitha commended for being "full of good works"unless works are important (Acts 9:36)?

3. According to the Second Letter of Peter, it is by striving to do good works that we are certain of our salvation (2 Peter 1:10).

4. Faith in the heart leads to justification, but it is *confession on the lips* that leads to salvation (Rom. 10:10). In other words, we must DO something and not simply believe. Recall, too, that "confession" in those days could mean martyrdom at the hands of both Jews and Romans.

5. Paul tells us emphatically that it is not enough to repent. One must do *works* befitting repentance (Acts 26:20).

6. Then there is Paul on love: "Though I have all faith so that I could remove mountains, and have not charity [i.e. works], I am nothing" (1 Cor. 13:2).

7.   John tells us that (a) that we will be cut off from the vine [of Christ] unless we bear fruit; (b) that we can't bear fruit unless we abide in Jesus; and (c) that we can't abide in Him unless we keep His commandments (John 15:1-11).

8.   When someone asked Jesus what was required for salvation, He did not say, "have faith" but rather, "Thou shalt not kill. Thou shalt not commit adultery. Thou shalt not steal." In other words, "Keep the commandments" (Mt. 19:16-19).

9.   In the Sermon on the Mount, the man whose right hand scandalizes him is bidden to cut it off (Hebraic hyperbole). Why is this necessary if he has faith?

10.   The man who builds his spiritual house on rock is the one who ACTS on what he hears (Luke 6:47-48). Why is this true if faith alone is all one needs?

11.   What is Jesus' "Depart from me, accursed ones, into everlasting fire, for I was hungry and you did not give me to eat" (Mt. 25:34-46) if not evidence of the need for works?

12.   The devil has faith in God, but he is not saved: "the devils also believe, and tremble" (James 2:19).

13.   According to Our Lord, we must lay up treasure for ourselves in heaven if this is where we want to go after death. And how does one do this? "Sell what thou hast," He tells the rich young man, and "give to the poor and thou shalt have treasure in heaven" (Mt. 19:21).

14. The last words of Jesus, as quoted by Matthew, are about the need to DO all that he commanded (Mt. 28:20).

15. There are also passages in Hebrew Scripture that point up the need for works – e.g. Jer. 17:10; Ez. 16:59; 18:21-29.

INDEX

About the Author

Holding a Ph.D. degree in history from the University of Michigan, as well as a BA degree from Holy Cross College (with 24 credits in theology and 18 in philosophy), Frederick Marks is both a speaking member of the Catholic Evidence Guild of New York and a coordinator for St. Paul Street Evangelization. As an author, he has written close to seventy articles, along with nine books, most recently *Think and Believe*. He has also appeared as a guest on EWTN's "Book Mark" and "Sunday Night Prime."